TM Wants You!

A Christian Response to Transcendental Meditation

by
David Haddon
and
Vail Hamilton

Baker Book House
Grand Rapids, Michigan

ISBN: 0-8010-4151-1
Copyright © 1976 Baker Book House Company

Contents

Acknowledgment

I would like to express my grateful acknowledgment for permission to publish material I have previously written on TM. Magazines and publishers include *Christianity Today, Eternity* (published by the Evangelical Foundation), and *His,* the magazine of Inter-Varsity Christian Fellowship. Inter-Varsity Press has also permitted extensive use of material from my booklet, *Transcendental Meditation: A Christian View.*

CHAPTER ONE

Transcendental Meditation: The Movement

by David Haddon and Vail Hamilton

QUESTION: Just what is TM?

ANSWER: Transcendental Meditation (TM) is the Eastern meditative practice taught by Maharishi Mahesh Yogi. TM is of special importance because the organized movement that has formed around it is by far the largest and fastest growing of the many Eastern spiritual disciplines that have taken root in the U.S. in recent years. TM has become so widespread that Maharishi's pleasant portrait may be seen everywhere from telephone-pole poster to color television screen. TM is the only one of these disciplines with sufficient breadth of appeal and general popularity to be of major national (and international) significance. The October 1975 *Time* cover story featuring Maharishi underlines the unique significance of TM in the spiritual life of America today.

When I was teaching TM in Berkeley in 1972, we

teachers told the public that TM is an effortless, scientifically verified technique for providing deep rest to the nervous system and unfolding the full mental potential of the individual. We denied that TM is a religion or a philosophy, claiming that its practice requires no prior faith commitment, no change of life-style or diet, and no special exercises. Maharishi and his organizations still present TM in similar terms. A letter from the Berkeley TM Center to parents of Bay Area high school students being offered TM through their public high school, for example, reads:

> TM is a natural, easy, systematic, and scientifically verified technique. It is not a religion or philosophy nor does it involve withdrawal from life.

Even in those days when I was teaching TM, I had a problem with my conscience about the way we pictured TM because I had entered TM when it was still frankly presented in spiritual terms. I knew, too, that *after* a person had committed himself financially by paying his initiation fee; ritually by bringing his flowers, fruit, and a clean white handkerchief to be offered to Guru Dev; and experientially by practicing the meditation three days, we would *then* let him know that he had taken the first steps toward the spiritual goal of Cosmic-consciousness. Maharishi justifies this approach on an elitist basis. In his verse-by-verse commentary, *Maharishi Mahesh Yogi on the Bhagavad-Gita,* he writes:

> If the enlightened man wants to bless one who is ignorant, he should ... try to lift him up from there by giving him the key to transcending [i.e., TM], so that he may gain bliss-consciousness and experience the Reality of Life. He should not tell him about the

level of the realized because it would only confuse him.[1]

For myself, I disregarded my conscience and accepted the deception involved because I then believed Maharishi's promise that if just 10 percent of the world's population practiced TM, world peace would be assured. The noble goal of world peace through widespread meditation seemed to justify the questionable means of lying. Regardless of the official denials of the religious character of TM, it is obvious that TM is a technique of mental yoga. And *yoga* is a Sanskrit word for "union." *Yoke*, for example, is a familiar English word from the same root. A yoke joins two animals in a unity. The yoking or union that is sought in all forms of yoga is the same; it is union with Divinity. Thus yoga, and with it TM, is religious in its very essence. Certainly, many people are practicing TM for other reasons. They are encouraged to do this by the way TM is presented in terms of its claimed physical and psychological benefits; but the goal of TM remains the same as that of all other systems of yoga. The consciousness is gradually and cumulatively altered so as to convince the yogi or meditator that he is experiencing his own divinity. In TM this is accomplished by silently reciting a "mantra" (a secret Sanskrit word) until perceptions and thoughts are eliminated from the mind and a passive state of mental awareness without any specific object is reached. This is to be repeated twice daily until the meditator reaches Cosmic-consciousness. If continued faithfully, TM will alter the normal state of consciousness, changing the very way in which reality is perceived.

The overtly religious aspect of the required initiation ceremony is partly concealed by the linguistic barrier of the Sanskrit language in which the *puja,* or hymn of worship, is sung by the teacher. Translation of the *puja* into English (see page 47) reveals that Maharishi's dead Master, Guru Dev ("Divine Leader") is worshiped in this ceremony as the very form of Brahma, Vishnu, and Shiva (the Hindu Trimurti), who are manifestations of the formless divinity of Brahman. Therefore TM has a strong, though publicly unacknowledged, element of devotional, or "bhakti," yoga.

To sum up, TM is a system of mantra yoga in which union with Divinity in an advanced state of Cosmic-consciousness is (in this lifetime) the ultimate though not commonly acknowledged goal. It also involves a strong element of "bhakti," or devotional yoga, which is imposed on every meditator through the required offerings that are presented to Guru Dev as to Divinity.

Since TM is presented by Maharishi and his personally trained teachers of TM as a nonreligious practice and since many people enter TM on this misleading basis, one purpose of this book will be to demonstrate the religious character of TM in some detail. This exposure of the deception upon which the growth and spread of TM has been based is a negative but necessary part of the larger purposes of this book. Another purpose is to compare the conflicting claims made by Eastern religion and Christian faith about the nature of God, man, and reality. Finally, we shall present the Lord Jesus Christ, the only Man in whom all the fullness of the Godhead dwells bodily, as the One through whom men and women can enjoy the fullness of life that some are seeking through Eastern meditative practices.

QUESTION: Where do TM and SCI come from?

ANSWER: Geographically and spiritually, TM and SCI come from the Far East. Maharishi Mahesh Yogi, who introduced TM to the West, is, of course, from India. The practice called TM and its underlying theory called "Science of Creative Intelligence" (SCI), while English in name, are both basically Indian in origin. A brief look at Maharishi's personal history will give some insight into the philosophical and spiritual baggage that he, as an itinerant holy man, carries with him on his world travels.

Maharishi Mahesh Yogi was born Mahesh Prasad Varma in 1918 in India. As a yogi, he retains only his family name of Mahesh. The title of "Yogi" means "one who practices yoga," whereas "Maharishi" means "great sage." Maharishi grew up as the son of a forest ranger. He attended the University of Allahabad from which he received a B.S. degree in physics in 1942. Shortly after graduation, he became a disciple of a guru called His Divinity Swami Brahmananda Saraswati, more commonly known as "Guru Dev." As a recluse in the mountains and forests of India, Guru Dev had gained such a reputation as a holy man that it is said that officials spent twenty years persuading him to accept the title and office of Shankaracharya of Jyotir Math, in Badarinath, India. This office made Guru Dev the honored head of the Hindu monastery, Jyotir Math, and one of the chief religious leaders of India. Guru Dev was 72 years old when he took office in 1941. The position of Shankaracharya there had been vacant for 150 years because no one had been considered worthy to be the spiritual leader of the people during that period. His time in office was considered propitious for India because she gained independence during his term. So great was his prestige in India that, according to the introduction to Maharishi's book *Love and God*, the first president of the Indian Union, Dr. Rajendra Prasad, and the second president, the noted Indian philosopher Dr. S. Rahdakrishnan, both actually worshiped Guru Dev.[2]

Maharishi's encounter with his Master, Guru Dev, came about in a strange, almost eerie way. He had been seeking a spiritual master for several years when one dark night a friend brought him to the house where Guru Dev was staying. After ascending a long flight of stairs to the front door, they asked to see Guru Dev; but they were told merely to wait on the veranda. After waiting in the darkness for some time, the headlights of a distant car illuminated the face of Guru Dev who had been sitting silently in the darkness all along. Instantly, Maharishi chose him as his spiritual Master.

Maharishi is said to have become his Master's favorite disciple because of his personal devotion ("bhakti") and service to Guru Dev. It is said that Maharishi would sometimes neglect to eat or sleep when finishing a task for his guru.

According to the tradition passed on to Maharishi from Guru Dev, the teaching of the practice of TM and of the knowledge of the Science of Creative Intelligence (SCI) passes through cycles of decline and revival following its initial revelation to holy men at the beginning of the cycle of creation in the form of the Vedas (Hindu Scriptures). One such revival of this supposed knowledge of reality is recorded in the *Bhagavad-Gita (Song of God)* in which the divine Being appears to the great warrior Arjuna in the form of Lord Krishna to reveal to him the right practice of yoga (TM, according to Maharishi). Later the practice of TM fell into decline again only to be rediscovered by the great Hindu philosopher-reformer Shankara. He established four monasteries in the north (that of Jyotir Math), south, east, and west of India as seats of learning to insure the permanence of the teaching and practice of TM. Despite Shankara's precautions, his teaching became distorted by ascetic withdrawal so that it was necessary for Guru Dev (an ascetic recluse) to rediscover the technique of TM as the means to integrate knowledge and devotion. Thus TM is held to be a revival of ancient wisdom lost to all the competing representatives of Hindu tradition as well as to all the other religions of the world.

However one regards this mixture of legend and history, it is apparent that Maharishi's teaching and practice come from a specific Hindu tradition. TM itself is represented as the correct means of yoga practice. SCI is supposed to be the wisdom of the Vedas rediscovered by Guru Dev and now scientifically verified by the direct experience of meditation and related research. Obviously, SCI is not a science in the understood sense, because it deals with an infinite and invisible "field of creative intelligence," the existence of which by its very nature cannot be verified by empirical observations of physical reality. Analysis will show that the presuppositions and conclusions of SCI largely coincide with those of Maharishi's Vedantic tradition of Hinduism. Though some clergymen have been slow to discern this eminently religious tradition in TM, journalists and scientists have recognized it as such. A writer for *Psychology Today,* for example, although sympathetic to TM nevertheless wrote of SCI that

13

the Science of Creative Intelligence, as it is called, is clearly a revival of ancient Indian Brahmanism and Hinduism. Its origins lie in the ancient texts—*Vedas, Upanishads, Bhagavad-Gita;* the teachings of the Buddha, and the synthesis of these traditions by Shankara.[3]

Maharishi's tradition, then, is that of the Vedantism of Shankara. Maharishi's guru held the title of "successor to Shankara," a Shankaracharya. Shankara was the ninth-century Hindu reformer who taught the absolute unity of all being (that "All is One"). Philosophically, this doctrine of universal oneness is called "monism." It is a variety of pantheism. Maharishi's SCI is largely a restatement in quasi-scientific language of Shankara's monism. When, for example, a TM teacher claims that there is a field of creative intelligence underlying all existence, he is merely using a new terminology for the impersonal intelligence of Brahman, or "Being," which is presumed to underlie all existence in the ancient monism of Shankara. Thus Hindu monism, a variety of pantheism, is the philosophy of the entire TM movement.

After the death of Guru Dev in 1953, Maharishi withdrew to a cave in the Himalayas. After two years of isolation there, Maharishi emerged and began teaching in south India. Early in 1959, he set out from India for the United States with the simple yogic technique of meditation now called "TM." By midsummer a branch of his Spiritual Regeneration Movement (SRM) was begun in Los Angeles. Since that time, about three-quarters of a million Americans have been initiated into TM. Maharishi has never had a large following in India where Hindu sages are commonplace and meditative practices abound. The headquarters of TM now is in Seelisberg, Switzerland,

14

and Maharishi seldom visits his native India. TM and its underlying philosophy of SCI are certainly Indian in origin, but their future fate will be determined in the West, which is subjecting them to scientific scrutiny. They must also be subjected to scrutiny in the light of the written Word of God, the Bible, to determine their ultimate value.

QUESTION: What organizations are promoting TM in the United States?

ANSWER: From 1959 to 1965, the Spiritual Regeneration Movement (SRM) was the only organization teaching TM in the United States. In 1965, interest began to grow among college students. The Student's International Meditation Society (SIMS) was formed to teach TM and the Science of Creative Intelligence (SCI) near high school and college campuses worldwide. In addition, the International Meditation Society (IMS) was formed for the general public, and the American Foundation for the Science of Creative Intelligence (AFSCI) was formed to arouse the interest of the business world. The fundamental teaching in all four organizations remains the same, but different benefits of TM are emphasized by each. The fifth branch of the movement, Maharishi International University (MIU), was founded in 1971 to train teachers and develop teaching materials and curricula for courses in the Science of Creative Intelligence.

A sixth organization, known as the World Plan Executive Council (WPEC), was formed to integrate the five organizations mentioned above. "WPEC" replaces "SIMS" as the official name of incorporation, which is in keeping with Maharishi's aim to deemphasize the religious aspects of TM and to promote his world goals.

All of these various organs of the TM movement are directly under Maharishi's control through a core group of 108 followers. They are financially independent and divide their time between being with Maharishi and working in the movement.

QUESTION: Who has provided leadership for Maharishi in the U.S.?

ANSWER: After having received a vision of the spiritual regeneration of all mankind from two years of solitude in the Himalaya Mountains, Maharishi began a series of world tours, coming to the United States in April 1959. The first to hear and respond to Maharishi's message were business and professional people. Gradually, they formed a branch of the Spiritual Regeneration Movement in Los Angeles to handle lecture and travel arrangements. Charlie Lutes, a top salesman for a construction firm, became president of SRM; and he still heads it.

Charlie Lutes has the reputation of being one of the most outspoken leaders of the TM movement. The initial promotion of TM by SRM was explicitly spiritual and SRM has retained much of this original emphasis. Generally, the sort of people who are attracted to SRM are upper-middle-class professional people whose interests lean toward the occult or the metaphysical. Charlie Lutes is a very popular lecturer among meditators, and he liberally sprinkles his lecture material with references to the Hindu philosophy and mystical aspects of TM.

Beulah Smith of San Diego is another well-known teacher and lecturer for TM. She was the only teacher of TM in the United States from 1961-1966. Maharishi was on his world travels at that time, lecturing and opening up centers in Canada, England, Germany, Sweden, India, Burma, Ceylon, east and South Africa, and Australia.

Jerry Jarvis of SIMS is Maharishi's "righthand man" in spreading and popularizing TM. He started to practice the technique in 1961. In 1966, he became a teacher of TM and was appointed director of SIMS and IMS. He is a full-time teacher and lecturer and is present at almost all of the teacher-training courses that Maharishi directs. I was personally taught by Jerry Jarvis in 1967 when the movement had just begun in the Berkeley campus area.

It is interesting to see that Jerry Jarvis had initial reservations about learning TM. Attracted by the name "Maharishi," which means "great holy sage," he and his wife Debby drove for an hour to get to a lecture on TM, but almost turned away when they found the admission charge was one dollar. Jerry says, "I had the idea that money should not be charged for spiritual things, but because we had driven so far to get there—over an hour—we started to rationalize." But Maharishi has a way of charming the doubtful and, impressed by Maharishi and what he said, they signed up.

Jerry attended a three-week course for training meditation guides on Catalina Island, and while Maharishi was on world tour, Jerry began giving introductory lectures. In 1962, Maharishi gave another two-week course at Catalina Island. Jerry and a few others were invited to be with Maharishi at Lake Arrowhead, California. This is where Maharishi made the tapes for the book, *The Science of Being and the Art of Living*, which was completed in a couple of months.

Originally, Jerry gave a series of introductory talks

on TM. Later they were reduced to two, which is now the standard format everywhere. In January 1966, Maharishi held the first International Teacher Training Course at the new Academy of Meditation beside the Ganges, in the foothills of the Himalayas. Jerry and his wife went for four months and came back as teachers of TM.

In 1969, the Associated Students of Stanford University (ASSU) nominated Jerry as ASSU professor for the year. As such, he was able to present the course of his choice and called it "The Science of Creative Intelligence." One of the largest responses to a new course in Stanford's history resulted. This course formally exposed the academic community to Maharishi's teaching.

Jerry's personality has a charismatic quality, and many have been won to TM by his influence. He is thoroughly dedicated to promoting the movement and is almost as tireless as Maharishi in doing so.

In 1970, after the SCI course at Stanford, the teacher-training course was moved from India to Estes Park, Colorado, where the facilities were larger; then extended to Mallorca in 1971 and to Fiuggi, Italy, where over two thousand people became teachers of TM. I was trained by Maharishi in Fiuggi.

QUESTION: How extensive is TM's penetration of American society by means of Maharishi's world plan?

ANSWER: The penetration of American society by Transcendental Meditation (TM) since its arrival in 1959 is remarkable. TM is an international movement, but by far its greatest success has been in the United States. It is the most popular of the many Eastern meditative practices imported during the 60s and early

70s. About three-quarters of a million Americans have been taught TM since 1965. Half a million of these, a substantial majority, have learned TM since the adoption of the World Plan by Maharishi in 1972.

Thirty thousand Americans a month were reportedly initiated into TM during 1975. Fees for initiation are $45, $65, and $125 for high school students, college students, and adults respectively. Maharishi's Student's International Meditation Society (SIMS) reportedly received $14,000,000 during the fiscal year ending September 30, 1974. At the reported rate of initiations (assuming an average fee of $100, SIMS' income from the initiation fees alone could reach $36,000,000 a year.

The expansion of TM in the United States and around the world is coordinated by an international organization called the "World Plan Executive Council" (WPEC) with headquarters in Seelisberg, Switzerland. National WPEC's have been established in each target country. Maharishi's World Plan, administered by the WPEC, has the ambitious purpose of making TM and SCI available to every person in the world. It calls for establishing 3,600 SCI Teacher Training Centers around the world—one center for every one million persons. The centers in turn are to train one teacher of SCI for every one thousand persons. With over 370 World Plan Centers already established, the United States easily exceeds its theoretical quota of 280 centers. And over six thousand Americans have been personally trained by Maharishi as teachers of TM. The World Plan obviously has been quite successful in the United States as far as its basic logistics are concerned. Its missionary purpose of taking Maharishi's teaching to the whole world is so far advanced here that America is the chief recruiting ground for TM teachers as well as the main source of funds to the movement worldwide.

The seven substantive goals of Maharishi's World Plan are:

1. To develop the full potential of the individual.
2. To improve governmental achievements.
3. To realize the highest ideal of education.
4. To maximize the intelligent use of the environment.
5. To solve the problems of crime, drug abuse, and all behavior that brings unhappiness to the family of man.
6. To bring fulfillment to the economic aspirations of individuals and society.
7. *To achieve the spiritual goals of mankind in this generation* (emphasis added).[4]

The seven goals of the World Plan are all inclusive. They cover, respectively, the personal, political, educational, ecological, social, economic, and spiritual aspects of life. Life in its totality falls within the scope of the World Plan. And while TM started in the United States with the Spiritual Regeneration Movement (SRM) as a personal, spiritual practice, Maharishi has shrewdly shifted the emphasis in the presentation of TM from the spiritual to the practical and scientific to evade both materialistic and religious resistance to his spiritual teaching. This approach also has permitted TM to obtain government support and a place in the curriculum of public schools that would probably be denied to it if it were presented in its former, spiritual terms.

GOVERNMENT AND THE WORLD PLAN

In his book, *Transcendental Meditation*, Maharishi explains that "whenever and wherever religion dominates the mass consciousness, transcendental deep meditation should be taught in terms of religion." Recognizing that religion hardly dominates the mass consciousness in the West today, Maharishi directs that "for the present ... this transcendental deep meditation should be made available for the peoples through the agencies of government. It is not the time when any effort to perpetuate a new and useful ideology without the help of governments can succeed."[5]

Maharishi's approach to presenting his teaching may be considered opportunistic, but it certainly has been successful. In its pursuit of governmental support for TM, Maharishi's WPEC has been rewarded by expressions of official approval from several states and from a number of cities. Maharishi has addressed the legislatures of Illinois, Michigan, New Hampshire, and Iowa. The House of Representatives of Illinois passed a Resolution (HR 677) in 1972, sponsored by William J. Murphy, providing "that all educational institutions ... be strongly encouraged to study the feasibility of courses in Transcendental Meditation and the Science of Creative Intelligence...." The Connecticut Legislature has also been reported to have expressed its approval of TM.

The Michigan Governor's Office of Drug Abuse in 1971 issued a letter supporting TM "as a positive and fruitful alternative to drug use and abuse." Governor Thomas Salmon of Vermont, and Governor Marvin Mandel of Maryland both issued World Plan Week Proclamations in November 1973. Governor Salmon of Vermont also sent a letter in support of Maharishi's program to more than five thousand state employees, to every state legislator, and to every school superintendent and principal. The mayor of Houston, Texas, Fred Hofheinz, proclaimed a "Science of Creative

Intelligence Week" in August of 1974 because "it has been shown through government-sponsored SCI programs that inner fulfillment and outer progress can be developed in the citizenry."

In 1975, U.S. Senator Mike Gravel (D-Alaska) introduced a measure (SR-64) that would have put the United States Congress on record as affirming that the seven goals of Maharishi's World Plan (see p. 20) are all attainable by means of Maharishi's SCI. Since the goals of the World Plan are essentially the elimination of all the ills of the human race, support of SR-64 required great faith in TM and SCI, which the majority of the Senate subcommittee considering the measure apparently lacked since the measure was not approved. Since only Maharishi's organization teaches SCI and TM, this measure—which concerns itself with the achievement of "the spiritual goals of mankind in this generation"—was thoroughly sectarian as well as visionary.

Nor has Maharishi's WPEC had to content itself with mere resolutions and proclamations of support. According to the *Time* cover story on Maharishi (October 13, 1975), seventeen research grants involving TM have been funded by the federal government. Included among such grants are the following:

1. Federal funds of $72,000 were granted by the National Institute of Alcohol Abuse and Alcoholism for training in TM for 30 alcoholics in the Washington, D.C. area.

2. Federal funds of $35,000 were provided for a Title III educational research program in New Jersey schools training 150 students in TM.

3. Federal and state funds totaling $29,000 went to the South County Regional Work-Study Program in Narragansett, Rhode Island, for training in TM.

4. Federal funds of $21,500 were granted by the National Institute of Health for training 130 high school teachers as instructors in SCI at Humboldt State College, California, during August 1972.

Ten U.S. senators and congressmen reportedly practice TM. Those who acknowledge the practice include Senator Charles Percy (R-Ill.) and Congressman Richard Nolan (D-Minn.). Senators who have entered favorable statements about Maharishi's programs in the *Congressional Record* include Adlai Stevenson III (D-Ill.) and John Tunney (D-Calif.). Tunney's laudatory statement about Maharishi International University (MIU) from the Congressional Record serves as a kind of quasi-official imprimatur on the concluding pages of the MIU Catalog on which it is reproduced in facsimile.

MIU AND THE WORLD PLAN

Maharishi International University (MIU) is a key element in fulfilling the World Plan. MIU occupies a 185-acre campus in Fairfield, Iowa, purchased for $2.5 million in 1974. Faculty, students, and even the janitors are said to practice TM. All students must qualify as teachers of TM before graduation. All courses are integrated by the monist world view of the Hindu philosopher-reformer Shankara and by the experience of TM that is held to directly verify Shankara's teaching. Of the two doctoral programs listed in the 1974 catalog, one is in the Hindu Scriptures, the Vedas, whereas the other is in the "Psychophysiology of Evolving Consciousness." This year (75-76), six hundred students are pursuing "enlightenment" at MIU. They are being formed into an elite band of missionaries committed to the mission of carrying out Maharishi's World Plan.

23

TM AND THE ACADEMIC WORLD

TM first gained wide popularity on college campuses in the late 60s even before the advent of Maharishi's World Plan in 1972. Instruction in TM has been offered to students on most campuses in the nation. SIMS claims that campus chapters have been active at more than a thousand U.S. colleges. The university credit course in SCI first taught at Stanford in 1970 by SIMS National Director Jerry Jarvis has since been offered at about fifty colleges, including Yale, Harvard, Notre Dame, the University of Colorado, and the University of California. TM has become popular also as a research project for psychologists and physiologists because of the mental and physical changes observed during meditation and the benefits claimed by meditators. Symposiums on SCI held at various universities have drawn the participation of many scientists and men of letters, including such notables as Buckminster Fuller and Marshall McLuhan.

A good example of the still limited, yet significant, extent of TM's influence in the academic world and of how a well-placed meditator can promote TM before an important audience is Maharishi's invitation to address the Twenty-eighth Annual Conference of the American Association for Higher Education at Chicago in 1973. Maharishi used the opportunity to urge the educators to add SCI to the curricula of their colleges. According to the *Saturday Review of Education* (May 1973), Maharishi was merely invited because one of the program committee members, Sydney Reisberg of the State University of New York in Albany, is a "confirmed meditator." By this means, Maharishi gained access to an extremely influential audience in their own bailiwick.

TM AND THE PUBLIC SCHOOLS

TM was first introduced as an extracurricular course at the high school level in Eastchester, New York, in January 1971, under the direction of public school superintendent Dr. Francis G. Driscoll. In the fall of 1971, the SCI course was introduced for regular credit at this school. The Dade County Public School System (Miami, Florida) offered the SCI course to twenty-two teachers in 1973 as a preparation to offering the SCI course to students there. TM is offered to these SCI students as an "optional lab." TM has been offered as a separate course in itself in some schools at levels as low as the primary grades. Up to the fall of 1975, about twenty-five high schools have offered SCI as a regular course. Introductory lectures offering TM on an extracurricular basis have been offered much more widely at schools where the integrated SCI/TM course has not been offered. SCI is the academic part of the course, and TM is considered to be the "laboratory" part.

Much of the impetus for the teaching of TM in public schools has come from preliminary research indicating that those who persist in meditation tend to reduce drug abuse. Since many drug abusers are not interested in practicing TM, and others drop out after starting, the notion that TM is an effective solution to the drug abuse problem is an illusion (see pp. 83-88).

Opposition to the teaching of SCI and TM in public schools on grounds that their religious aspects violate constitutional guarantees against sectarian indoctrination at public expense has emerged, notably in California and New Jersey. These developments are discussed in the next question (p. 31).

TM AND THE MILITARY

The reputation of TM as a drug abuse control measure was also a major reason for the adoption of TM by the military. Major General Franklin M. Davis, Jr. became a meditator and promoted TM for drug abuse control while he was director of military personnel policies in the office of the Deputy Chief of Staff of the Army in 1971. His successor in the job, Brigadier General Robert Gard, also became a meditator in 1972, and included TM in the army's alcohol and drug abuse program. TM centers have been established at military bases, including Fort Dix, New Jersey; Fort Bliss, Texas; and at the Strategic Air Command Base in Omaha, Nebraska. At Fort Lewis, Washington, an instructor was actually hired by the 9th Infantry Division to present TM to drug and alcohol abusers in 1973.

According to the SIMS-IMS January-February 1976 "T.M. Newsletter":

> The United States military academy at West Point, New York, has offered courses in the Transcendental Meditation technique regularly for the past year. The Chief of Personnel Services Division at West Point, Lt. Col. Dudley L. Tadomy, said, "The initial response has been excellent. Cadets have reported the Transcendental Meditation programme has helped them to cope with the pressures of cadet life and with the strenuous academic regime."

TM AND BIG BUSINESS

The American Foundation for the Science of Creative Intelligence (AFSCI) was formed to take the mesage of TM to business corporations. It is claimed that TM increases efficiency and job satisfaction among employees and is even more helpful in relieving the tensions of managers. AFSCI has succeeded in convincing large corporations like AT&T and General Foods to offer the TM course to their employees. Favorable articles have appeared in a few business journals and in company periodicals, such as *Industry Week, California Business,* and *Hughes News.* Board Chairman Rick Polk of Packaging Associates Medical Corporation writes in one of a number of testimonial letters circulated by SIMS that "I heartily recommend Transcendental Meditation to the executives of those companies wishing greater productivity as a result of increased energy and efficiency from those employees practicing TM." AFSCI claims that some fifty corporations have provided instruction in TM for employees.

TM AND PSYCHIATRY

Dr. Bernard Glueck of the Institute for Living, a psychiatric institution at Hartford, Connecticut, and Dr. Harold Bloomfield, Clinical Director of Psychiatry at the Institute of Psychophysiological Medicine in El Cajon, California, are two psychiatrists who have risen to national prominence as aggressive proponents of TM. Bloomfield is a teacher of TM and co-author of a best-selling book promoting TM. Psychotherapists of an eclectic bent may accept TM as a convenient technique of relaxation, but Bloomfield is much more optimistic. The book he co-authored implicitly presents TM as replacement for traditional psychotherapy. The authors write, "We suggest that the practice of TM offers an alternative, not necessarily to replace the interpersonal encounter which is the core of psychotherapy, but as a significant means of reducing tension, broadening awareness and making life more meaningful and pleasurable, and *there-*

27

by fulfilling the goals of all forms of therapy" (emphasis added). If TM itself fulfills the "goals of all forms of therapy," it can easily replace them.

TM AND MEDICINE

Physiologist Robert K. Wallace (a meditator who is now President of Maharishi International University) and Harvard cardiologist Herbert Benson pioneered research into the physiological effects of TM. They also noted a statistical correlation between continuing practice of TM and reduced drug use. Benson has studied the use of TM as a measure to control high blood pressure. Other possible medical benefits claimed on the basis of preliminary research are relief from allergies and asthma; reduced susceptibility to infectious diseases; relief from insomnia; and reduced dependence upon alcohol, cigarettes, and other drugs. Since the psychosomatic nature of most of these illnesses makes them very difficult to treat medically, it is not surprising that some doctors are already prescribing TM and some are becoming meditators themselves. Dr. David W. Doner, assistant chief of the Renal Section at Boston Veteran's Administration Hospital, for example, recommends TM to some patients and has studied under Maharishi to become a teacher of TM.

TM AND PRISONER REHABILITATION

Prisons have been prominent among the institutions in which experimental programs involving TM have been tried. The *Harvard Law Record* of March 1974 records five pilot projects in federal and state prisons then underway or completed. Favorable articles on the possible use of TM in criminal justice reform and prisoner rehabilitation have also appeared in the *Ken-*

tucky Law Journal (1971-1972) and the *University of Maryland Law Forum* (Winter 1973).

THE MEDIA MAGNIFIES MAHARISHI

Maharishi has had a remarkably good press until quite recently when the very success of the movement has drawn both cynical and serious criticism from several sources. Favorable feature articles on TM have appeared in many magazines ranging from *Mademoiselle* to *Soldier's* (the official U.S. Army Magazine). Academic, scientific, and business journals have also published favorable reports along with occasional adverse comments and a few critical articles. In 1972, both the *New York Times* and the *Wall Street Journal* published long articles on TM, which were widely reprinted by SIMS to promote TM. *Time* devoted its October 13, 1975 cover story to Maharishi.

Most journalists writing about TM take up its practice, to report on it knowledgeably. They generally do not consider that practicing TM may impair their objectivity as reporters. Many of these writers simply accept uncritically the view of TM as a nonreligious technique of relaxation presented to them in the introductory lecture. Their articles often are little more than personal testimonials to their favorable impression of TM and a presentation of the official SIMS explanation of TM and its benefits.

A major breakthrough on commercial television was made by Maharishi in April of 1975, when he was interviewed by Merv Griffin (a new and enthusiastic meditator) on Griffin's talk show. Other guests giving testimonials for TM on that show were TV actress Ellen Corby (Grandma Walton), California State Senator Arlen Gregorio, and psychiatrist-TM teacher Harold Bloomfield. Audience impact of this show may have been the greatest media boost Maharishi had received up to that time. Because of its great success, another show was taped for release on Halloween 1975. Special guests for the second show were film actor Clint Eastwood, television personality Mary Tyler Moore, psychiatrist Dr. Bernard Glueck, and Minnesota Congressman Richard N. Nolan.

In addition to favorable publicity on commercial TV via programs like the "Merv Griffin Show," the WEPC has recently gained educational TV channels on both coasts of the United States. These stations can broadcast the video-taped lectures of Maharishi presenting the principles of the Hindu monism of Shankara as the Science of Creative Intelligence. They may also develop programs with meditating performers and celebrities such as singers Stevie Wonder and Peggy Lee; musician Smokey Robinson; and sports stars Joe Namath, Bill Walton, and Craig Lincoln.

Several books favorable to TM have appeared in recent years in addition to those written by Maharishi and his close followers. It was in 1975, however, that Maharishi's writing followers began to hit publishing pay dirt in a big way with two nationwide best sellers. In hard cover, *TM: Discovering Inner Energy and Overcoming Stress* by Harold Bloomfield (the already-mentioned psychiatrist-TM teacher), Michael Cain, and Dennis Jaffe was among the top ten best sellers for much of the year. In soft cover, another best seller was the *TM Book* by Denise Denniston and Peter McWilliams. They attempt a whimsical approach to their aggressive purpose of getting the reader out of his middle-class mind-set just enough to try something different: TM.

TM AND THE CLERGY

TM has not failed to gain adherents and apologists from the ranks of the clergy. In the *TM Book* just referred to, for example, there are testimonial letters from a Jewish rabbi, a Lutheran theologian, and a Catholic priest, recommending the practice of TM as compatible with their faiths. One Catholic priest, who is director of a parochial high school in Springfield, Massachusetts, approved the teaching of SCI and TM in his high school after he became a meditator. Other Christian clergymen, however, have vigorously opposed TM as a practice contrary to Christian faith. These shepherds consider the offerings and homage given to the picture of Guru Dev in the initiation ceremony to be idolatrous and the underlying doctrine explaining TM to be pantheistic.

QUESTION: Has there been effective opposition to the TM movement?

ANSWER: There have been occasional critical comments and articles about Maharishi or TM by scientists, scholars, and writers, but these have been relatively few and ineffective in influencing public opinion. The main source of sustained critical interest in and opposition to TM has been the Christian community. Initially, Christians as a group were slow to become aware of the existence of TM. As young people from the counter-culture were being converted to the Christian faith in the late 60s and early 70s, however, they included a number of those who had been into TM. These vital, young Christians testified to an opposition between the living Christ within them and the spirit of TM. An intuitive sense of this conflict between Christian faith and TM typically led them to drop the practice of TM spontaneously even when they were not counseled to do so on Biblical grounds. As awareness of TM and of its inner character has grown in the Christian community, Christian writers, pastors, and theologians have pointed out the Biblical reasons for the intuitive rejection of TM by Christians sensitive to the Holy Spirit.

As TM slowly began to be introduced to fill the spiritual vacuum of the secularized public school system in the early 70s, the stage was set for a confrontation between the Christian community and Maharishi's movement. The issue was taken up by Christians in California in 1973 over a state assembly resolution promoting the teaching of SCI and TM in California schools sponsored by Assemblyman Ken Meade (D-Oakland). The Resolution (ACR66) would have resolved that "the Legislature strongly encourages the inclusion of courses in the science of creative intelligence on the campuses and in the facilities of all educational institutions. . . ." A similar legislative resolution had been passed in Illinois in 1972. A majority of the California Assembly Education Committee present and voting approved the measure in May 1973, but the required number of yeas from the seventeen-member committee was not then attained. The measure was therefore set aside for possible reconsideration.

In July of that year, Christian World Liberation Front (CWLF), under the leadership of Jack Sparks, caught wind of this resolution through a Berkeley TM Center Newsletter. CWLF sent a personal letter opposing ACR66 to each member of the Assembly Education Committee along with a copy of a staff report showing evidence of the religious aspects of SCI and TM. The letter contended that teaching of TM and

SCI in public schools violated traditional American freedom from sectarian indoctrination at public expense.

In Sacramento, the representatives of Maharishi had not been idle. According to TM instructor Peter Georgi, SIMS offered all seventeen members of the California Assembly Education Committee personal instruction in TM and about half of them accepted the offer and began practicing TM.

By the late fall of 1973, straight and counter-cultural Christians in the Bay Area had joined forces against ACR66 by forming the Christian Joint Education Committee. Walnut Creek Presbyterian Church and CWLF sponsored the committee to inform the Christian community of the challenge of TM to Christian faith and to inform as wide an audience as possible of the political aspects of the invasion of the schools by a new religious teaching (SCI) and practice (TM).

The writers of this book had a brief opportunity to share with Assemblyman Meade our view of the conflict between TM and Christian faith at a Democratic Club meeting in 1973. Vail told Meade that she had given up teaching TM for something better, Jesus Christ. Meade expressed surprise that Vail had abandoned TM as contrary to her Christian faith. Apparently, Meade had not previously heard of the conflict between TM and Christianity.

Meade's resolution finally died in committee late in January of 1974, apparently because Meade lacked the votes to have it approved. The first major confrontation between the Christian community and the TM movement thus concluded with a quiet victory for the outspoken representatives of Christian faith. Because of the likelihood of such results, Maharishi's representatives prefer to avoid such confrontation by working quietly behind the scenes with politicians and by denying that there are any grounds for conflict between TM and any religion.

In New Jersey, yet another state assembly resolution (AR47) encouraging the study of TM by state officials was considered in 1975. AR47 was also expected to die in committee because of a mountain of opposing mail. At the local level, the issue of the teaching of TM in the public schools was joined in Newton, New Jersey, in August of 1974. Rev. Robert Craig, assistant pastor of Lafayette Federated Church, cited before the Newton School Board passages from Maharishi's writings showing the Hindu basis of TM. School Superintendent Dr. S. David Adler withdrew his recommendation of TM for the schools *after* Rev. Craig's revelation of the religious aspect of TM caused the school board to refuse even to vote on the issue.

The controversy over the teaching of TM in public schools finally led to legal action against a California school district in which SCI and TM had been taught. Lutheran Pastor William Grunow filed a class action suit in the Superior Court for the County of Alameda against the San Lorenzo Unified School District for expenditures of funds that have supported the doctrine, practice, and religion taught by Maharishi. The suit arose as a result of the teaching of TM at Bohannon Junior High School involving fourteen seventh graders during 1974-1975 and of the teaching of an SCI course at San Lorenzo High School. According to the Berkeley Christian Coalition (formerly CWLF) Spiritual Counterfeits Project, the defendant, the San Lorenzo School District, had planned to teach a course in SCI again this year if student interest were sufficient. In view of the lawsuit, however, the school district filed a declaration with the judge promising not to recommend the teaching of TM and to oppose such classes if they were again proposed. As a result, SCI and TM have been banished from a school district where they had been taught. A legal precedent is still lacking, however, since the court found it unnecessary to rule on the plaintiff's suit in view of the defendant's promise not to teach TM in the future.

In New Jersey, a group called Coalition for Religious Integrity (CRI) has brought suit in U.S. Federal Court against defendants Maharishi Mahesh Yogi, five branches of the TM movement (SIMS, IMS, WPEC, AFSCI, and SRM), the State of New Jersey, and the United States Government. CRI contends that the $40,000 in federal funds being used to finance the teaching of TM in four Newark area public high schools violates the First Amendment provision against sectarian teaching at public expense. CRI attorney John E. Patton, a Roman Catholic, expects that the issue will be brought quickly to the U.S. Supreme Court if there is an appeal. It is to be hoped that the New Jersey case will bring a definitive judgment both against teaching TM in the schools and federal support of such programs.

Perhaps an even more serious threat to the TM organization may come in the form of consumer fraud suits. According to *Christian Century's* special correspondent Robert Brank Fulton, a Fairfield, Iowa (home of MIU) clergyman named Charles Sloca has requested that the state attorney take action against the TM organization for violation of the consumer's right to know the true nature of a service offered. Sloca claims that TM is being sold as a scientific technique whereas it is really a religious practice. The prospect of a consumer fraud suit must be a nightmare for WPEC officials because it might mean that any initiate of TM could demand repayment of his initiation fee. Such a judgment would definitively expose the deception on which the marketing of TM has been founded. It could also quickly dismantle the financial basis of the empire Maharishi has built in the United States.

From the above examples it is apparent that effective opposition to the political and educational initiatives of Maharishi's movement has largely been the work of Christians. They have recognized its fundamentally religious character and have been sensitive to the spiritual and philosophical dimensions of Maharishi's teaching when others have not been.

TM: Its Prospects

In view of the extent of the organization that Maharishi has built in the United States and around the world in the last seventeen years, he must be taken seriously as a shrewd and dedicated leader. It is apparent from the brief account in the previous question that convinced meditators hold important positions in government, the academic world, the public schools, the military, big business, psychiatry, medicine, the media, entertainment, sports, and religion. Their numbers are still relatively small, but many of them are willing to use their influence to promote TM because they believe it has benefited them personally and because they are convinced that it provides an answer to social and political problems as well. Maharishi's WPEC itself appears to operate as a well-oiled international corporation on the basis of its large American revenues and the frugal life-style of the typical TM teacher who is dedicated to the transformation of mankind through TM, with the goal of world peace through Maharishi's World Plan.

The prospects, then, for a massive and continuing expansion of the practice of TM in the United States would seem to be excellent except for one thing: the contradiction between the public presentation of TM as a nonreligious technique of relaxation and the private reality of TM as a religious practice and spiritual path. Maharishi's shrewd opportunism in shifting from a spiritual to a scientific emphasis in the presentation of TM led him to make a total public denial of the religious aspects of TM. As these aspects are being exposed to public view by the publication of such material as the translation of the English text of the Sanskrit hymn of worship to Guru Dev and the Hindu divinities used in the initiation of every meditator, Maharishi's credibility as a spiritual leader is being undermined.

Even though many people are willing to ignore the deceptions of a Watergate in government or religion so long as their own interests seem to be served, there is a Providence that brings such matters to light. That Providence appears to be working against Maharishi's empire today just as it worked against the Nixon administration in the recent past. If this estimate proves true, the prophetic word of Isaiah may be applied to Maharishi's worldwide spiritual empire:

> Do you not know, Have you not heard?
> Has it not been declared to you from the beginning?
> . . . He it is who reduces rulers to nothing,
> Who makes the judges of the earth meaningless.
> Scarcely have they been planted,
> Scarcely have they been sown,
> Scarcely has their stock taken root in the earth,

But He merely blows on them, and they wither,
And the storm carries them away like stubble.

(Isaiah 40:21, 23-24 NASB)

Notes

1. Maharishi, *On the Bhagavad-Gita: A New Translation and Commentary* (Baltimore: Penguin Books, 1967), p. 224.
2. Maharishi, *Love and God* (Los Angeles: MIU Press, 1973), p. 9.
3. Colin Campbell, "The Facts on Transcendental Meditation, Part I," *Psychology Today,* April 1974, p. 38.
4. Anonymous, *An Address to Governments* (Los Angeles: Maharishi International University, 1972), p. 24.
5. Maharishi, *Transcendental Meditation: The Science of Being and Art of Living* (New York: New American Library, 1963), pp. 299-300.

CHAPTER TWO

Transcendental Meditation: The Practice

by Vail Hamilton

QUESTION: Just what does a person do while meditating in TM?

ANSWER: The meditator usually sits on a chair in a normal posture with hands folded and eyes closed. He repeats his personal mantra (a secret Sanskrit word) over and over silently until it slips from his attention. As soon as the meditator notices he is off the mantra, he simply returns to the mantra and resumes repetition. This is done for twenty minutes both morning and evening.

From personal experience I can describe just what TM was like for me. My meditations were almost always easy. Some seemed deeper than others, but nothing unusual or even profound seemed to happen during meditation for the first few years. The noticeable changes that were going on, except for the relaxation, occurred during the rest of the day rather than during meditation. I would emerge from TM feeling refreshed, energized, and calmer. I no longer felt the desire to take a nap in the afternoon because TM would give me the relaxation I seemed to need. During the two weeks prior to receiving my mantra at the initiation into TM, we were told to abstain from drugs not prescribed by a doctor. I had taken several LSD trips a few years earlier and occasionally smoked marijuana. The TM teachers told us that we would find our desire for any kind of "recreational" drugs disappearing as we got high with TM. This claim proved true in my experience. I lost all appetite for pot because, compared with TM, it seemed to lower my awareness rather than raise it.

Other effects of TM in my life were more unusual and raise unsettling questions about the practice. Many times when I was meditating, for example, I would "come to" an hour or so later, having fallen asleep. Sometimes during meditation a lapse of consciousness, during which I could recall nothing later, would occur. These lapses are referred to as the "blackout phenomenon" and are not discussed publicly. Maharishi explains "blackouts" during TM as an experience of transcendence, but no one really knows what actually happens.

Not everyone who practices TM finds it completely relaxing. Some meditators find themselves becoming tense and anxious as a result of TM. This effect of TM is referred to as "unstressing." The official explanation for unstressing is that the nervous system is throwing off a lot of stress and it is coming out in uncomfortable ways. Some people have severe physical and emotional effects from "unstressing," such as epileptic seizures, skin eruptions, anger, and hostility. The TM organizations never publicly warn of the dangers involved in the practice of TM, but from my personal knowledge I can state that "unstressing" has been accompanied by heart seizures and psychotic behavior. At the long meditation retreats "unstressing" is a common problem because the long cycles of hatha yoga exercises *(asanas)*, breathing exercises *(pranayama)*, and TM (together called "rounding") combine to trigger it. At these "rounding courses," severe cases of "unstressing" often had to be treated with hot baths, foot massage, zone therapy, and cutting down of the number of hours spent in meditation.

TM teachers suffer more of the distressing effects of "unstressing" than others because they spend more time in meditation and because of the peculiar effect of the initiation ceremony itself upon the teachers who must repeat it every time a new meditator is initiated. The initiation ceremony includes a hymn that is sung in Sanskrit; this hymn is in itself an extended mantra which speeds up the process of consciousness alteration. I got "high" every time I initiated a new meditator just from the effects of the hymn and ceremony. Sometimes I would have to lie down between initiations because they made me feel heavy and sleepy, almost as though I had been drugged. Some teachers said that they would see visions of Maharishi and Guru Dev and other masters while performing the ceremony.

I experienced the emotional effects of "unstressing" from time to time, especially at teacher training courses or long retreats where more time than usual was spent in meditation. Feelings of loneliness, despair, and anger surfaced occasionally and were difficult to cope with because no one wanted to hear about it or be around anyone with "bad vibes." At times like that, I felt that TM was just a cold, heartless rat race to Cosmic-consciousness. At other times, however, I felt incredibly high and blissful. Then I would be optimistic about where TM was leading me.

QUESTION: What is the mantra?

ANSWER: In TM the mantra is a word or sound from Sanskrit, the sacred language of the Hindu scriptures. These mantras are presented to meditators as meaningless sounds. In Sir John Woodruffe's book on mantras, *The Garland of Letters,* however, it is revealed that "every letter, syllable and mantra is . . . a form of the Brahman."[1] And Brahman is formless deity which may manifest either as a god or goddess. Therefore, even those mantras that are not explicitly the names of a god invoke deity in one form or another. My first mantra was not the name of a specific god, though my advanced-technique mantra was. This distinction makes little difference, however, since both mantras invoke deity. In *Meditations of Maharishi Mahesh Yogi,* he describes the mantras in spiritual terms:

> The entire knowledge of the mantras or hymns of the Vedas is devoted to man's connection, to man's communication with the higher beings in different strata of creation.[2]

Here Maharishi verifies Woodruffe's statement that the sound of the mantras has religious significance.

Elsewhere, however, Maharishi defines a mantra merely as "a sound, the effects of which are known."[3] Different sounds are supposed to have different effects on the nervous system. The impression has even been given that the mantras are assigned on the basis of personal qualities of the initiate. Selection of the mantras is really quite mechanical; it is based on statistical information from the questionnaire the candidate fills out when applying for initiation. When I was teaching TM, I had a list of about fifteen mantras from which to select the "right" mantra for every person I initiated. Maharishi gave each teacher a list of mantras. We were told to keep the list secret; teachers were not even supposed to compare their lists with each other. I do not know whether the same list of mantras was given to each teacher or not.

Repetition of a mantra is one of the standard means of inducing the classical mystical experience of unity. The technique and the experience seem to be common to various mystical traditions of both East and West. The Biblical tradition, however, makes no use of mantras and records no instance of the unitive mystical experience. The striking experiences of God recorded by the prophets and the apostles were characterized not by their sense of unity with the essence of God, but by the sense of His otherness tempered by His loving verbal communication. Rather than the inexpressible subjective experience of union of the mystic, they received prophetic words of truth from God, which they were commissioned to speak to others. Christ Himself specifically condemns the use of a mantra when He forbids "vain repetition" as a pagan practice not to be used by His followers (Matt. 6:7).

QUESTION: How does a person start meditating?

ANSWER: Here is the general procedure for instruction in TM:

1. Introductory lecture (1 hr.)
2. Preparatory lecture (1 hr.)

3. Interview (5 min.)
4. Personal instruction (1½-2 hrs.). Initiation ceremony.
5. Workshop (1½-2 hrs.) "Practical Consideration of TM."
6. Workshop (1½-2 hrs.) "Mechanics of Stress Reduction."
7. Workshop (1½-2 hrs.) "The Realization of Full Mental Potential Through Transcendental Meditation and the Science of Creative Intelligence." (Cosmic-consciousness as a spiritual goal.)

The two lectures introducing TM are free. During the personal interview with the teacher, the candidate fills out an information sheet and answers such questions as name, age, occupation or school, past or present experience with drugs, psychotherapy, religion, or other meditation techniques. During the interview, a time is arranged for the personal instruction, usually on a Saturday, and the candidate is told to bring a clean white handkerchief, three pieces of sweet fruit, and several fresh flowers. The personal instruction includes the initiation ceremony. Two days later, after approximately four meditations have elapsed, everyone from the particular group will meet for a two-hour workshop that meets on three consecutive nights. Course fees range from $35.00 for a grade school student to $125.00 for a working adult. During the workshop of the last day, the spiritual goal of Cosmic-consciousness is revealed and discussed.

Now I will describe briefly what is said during the two free lectures given to the general public. In the introductory lecture, the teacher starts out by saying what TM is thought *not* to be. TM is considered not to be a method of concentration or contemplation or mental control; not a religion or a particular way of life; and not something you must believe in for it to work. Then TM is described in terms of what it *is* considered to be: a simple effortless technique giving profound rest and bringing greater creativity to the mind and life of the practitioner. Unfoldment of mental potential is related to contacting the deepest level of the mind, which is postulated as an infinite field of energy, intelligence, and creativity. The teacher compares TM to scientific fields such as physics and psychobiology, and discusses experiments done on TM meditators and some of the results on the body, such as breathing, heart rate, and brain patterns. Then TM is related to social benefits, such as improved grades in school, better interpersonal relations, and reduced crime rates.

The preparatory (second) lecture starts with an overall review of the previous lecture material and then the technique itself is examined in more detail. The teacher describes what a mantra is and its effects on the consciousness of the meditator. He refers to the Vedic tradition from which TM comes and shows the framed picture of Guru Dev, explaining that he is Maharishi's master, the last great custodian of this tradition. The seven steps of instruction are outlined and explained. Then the teacher finishes up with a general discussion of the governmental and educational interest in TM and the establishment of Maharishi International University and the SCI course that is being offered (Science of Creative Intelligence). The teacher discusses course fees for TM and asks that no drugs be taken for the two weeks prior to initiation.

The initiation ceremony is a required procedure

in learning TM. The candidate is instructed to bring an offering of six flowers, three pieces of fresh fruit, and a clean white handkerchief to the meditation center. There the candidate is asked to remove his shoes, after which he is brought into a small candle-lit room filled with incense. Then his offering is placed upon an altar before a framed picture of Guru Dev ("Divine Leader") who is Maharishi's departed master. The candidate is asked to stand before the altar while the teacher sings the *puja* in Sanskrit. This *puja* is a Sanskrit hymn of praise and worship. It is the heart of the initiation ceremony. Only after it has been chanted is the initiator free to impart the mantra to the would-be meditator.

The meaning of the *puja* is not revealed to the candidate who cannot understand it unless he happens to speak Sanskrit. The translation of the *puja* that appears below is taken from *The Holy Tradition,* a handbook issued to all teachers of TM. Commenting on the first part of the *puja,* this handbook reads: "The purpose of this invocation is to attune the active mind by directing it towards the great Masters, to the essential nature of their knowledge of Absolute being."[4] Thus the *puja* is intended to alter the consciousness of both instructor and candidate in a way that opens the mind to the influence of the "great Masters." Its function is understood to be the establishment of a spiritual or psychic bond between the new meditator on the one hand and Maharishi and his Hindu tradition of Masters on the other.

Though the translation of the *puja* was a well-kept secret until its publication by Berkeley Christian Coalition (formerly CWLF) in 1975, Maharishi's organizations may now be forced to make the translation of the *puja* available to initiates to avoid consumer fraud suits on the basis of the "nonreligious" claim made for TM. The religious character of the *puja* is inescapable.

The *puja* is presented in three parts. The first stage is a recitation of the names of gods and personages representing the line of succession through which the secret knowledge of the mantras has passed, up until the most recently deceased spiritual master, Maharishi's guru, Brahmananda Sarasvati (Guru Dev). Each person mentioned in the *puja* is considered to be a fully realized expression of divinity and is therefore thought worthy of worship.

Invocation
Whether pure or impure, whether purity or impurity is permeating everywhere, whoever opens himself to the expanded vision of unbounded awareness gains inner and outer purity.

Invocation
To LORD NARAYANA, to lotus-born BRAHMA the Creator, to VASHISHTHA, to SHAKTI and his son PARASHAR, to VYASA, to SHUKADEVA, to the great GAUDAPADA, to GOVINDA, ruler among the yogis, to his disciple, SHRI SHANKARACHARYA, to his disciples PADMA PADA and HASTA MALAKA and TROTAKACHARYA and VARTIKA-KARA, to others, to the tradition of our Masters, I bow down. To the abode of the wisdom of the SHRUTIS, SMRITIS and PURANAS, to the abode of kindness, to the personified glory of the LORD, to SHANKARA, emancipator of the world, I bow down. To SHANKARACHARYA the redeemer, hailed as KRISHNA and BADARAYANA, to the commentator of the BRAHMA SUTRAS, I bow down. To the glory of the Lord I bow down again and again, at whose door the whole galaxy of gods pray for perfection day and night. Adorned with im-

measurable glory, preceptor of the whole world, having bowed down to Him we gain fulfillment. Skilled in dispelling the cloud of ignorance of the people, the gentle emancipator, BRAHMANANDA SARASVATI, the supreme teacher, full of brilliance, Him I bring to my awareness.

The second part of the *puja* is an offering of different items to the spiritual master, Guru Dev, accompanied by the words, "I bow down." At this point the candidate's fruit, flowers, and handkerchief, which he has been instructed to bring, are placed on the altar and presented in a ritualized manner.

> Offering the invocation to the lotus feet of SHRI GURU DEV, I bow down.
> Offering a seat to the lotus feet of SHRI GURU DEV, I bow down.
> Offering an ablution to the lotus feet of SHRI GURU DEV, I bow down.
> Offering cloth to the lotus feet of SHRI GURU DEV, I bow down.
> Offering sandalpaste to the lotus feet of SHRI GURU DEV, I bow down.
> Offering full rice to the lotus feet of SHRI GURU DEV, I bow down.
> Offering a flower to the lotus feet of SHRI GURU DEV, I bow down.
> Offering incense to the lotus feet of SHRI GURU DEV, I bow down.
> Offering light to the lotus feet of SHRI GURU DEV, I bow down.
> Offering water to the lotus feet of SHRI GURU DEV, I bow down.
> Offering fruit to the lotus feet of SHRI GURU DEV, I bow down.
> Offering water to the lotus feet of SHRI GURU DEV, I bow down.

Offering a betel leaf to the lotus feet of SHRI GURU
DEV, I bow down.
Offering a coconut to the lotus feet of SHRI GURU
DEV, I bow down.

The last part of the *puja* is a hymn of praise to the
supposed deity of Guru Dev and is an overt act of
religious worship. Guru Dev is identified with the
three gods of the Hindu Trimurti—Brahma, Vishnu,
and Shiva—as the "personified fulness of Brahman."

Offering a camphor light

White as camphor, kindness incarnate, the essence of
creation garlanded with BRAHMAN, ever dwelling
in the lotus of my heart, the creative impulse of cosmic life, to That, in the form of GURU DEV, I bow
down. Offering light to the lotus feet of SHRI GURU
DEV, I bow down. Offering water to the lotus feet
of SHRI GURU DEV, I bow down.

Offering a handful of flowers

GURU in the glory of BRAHMA, GURU in the
glory of VISHNU, GURU in the glory of the great
LORD SHIVA, GURU in the glory of the personified transcendental fulness of BRAHMAN, to Him,
to SHRI GURU DEV adorned with glory, I bow
down. The Unbounded, like the endless canopy of the
sky, the omnipresent in all creation, by whom the sign
of That has been revealed, to Him, to SHRI GURU
DEV, I bow down. GURU DEV, SHRI BRAH-
MANANDA, bliss of the Absolute, transcendental
joy, the Self-Sufficient, the embodiment of pure knowledge which is beyond and above the universe like the
sky, the aim of "Thou are That" and other such expressions which unfold eternal truth, the One, the
Eternal, the Pure, the Immoveable, the Witness of all
Intellects, whose status transcends thought, the Transcendent along with the three gunas, the true preceptor,

to SHRI GURU DEV, I bow down. The blinding
darkness of ignorance has been removed by applying
the balm of knowledge. The eye of knowledge has
been opened by Him and therefore, to Him, to SHRI
GURU DEV, I bow down. Offering a handful of
flowers to the lotus feet of SHRI GURU DEV, I bow
down.[5]

At the very end of the *puja* the teacher invites the
participant to kneel before the altar for a few moments
of silence, and then, both still kneeling, the teacher
repeats the mantra selected for the initiate and has
him repeat it until correctly pronounced. They then
sit down for further instruction. After this, the initiate is brought into another room where he will experience his first twenty-minute meditation.

TM representatives insist that the initiation ceremony is nonreligious because it does not involve a
faith commitment from the candidate. But it is obvious that there is both active and passive involvement
in the religious ceremony by the candidate. He must,
at a minimum, bring his offerings, pay the fee, and
attend the ritual before receiving his mantra.

Several candidates I encountered while teaching
TM objected to this religious aspect but went along
with it to learn the technique. A friend of mine who
is a teacher of TM once told me that the initiation
ceremony freaked her out so much because of her
Jewish religion that prohibits bowing down before
anyone but God Almighty, that she literally ran out
of the initiation room. Her instructor managed to talk
her into at least witnessing the ceremony, and today
she laughs about the incident. For me, by contrast, the
whole ceremony had such an outward appearance of
godliness, and was linked to such a charming experience, that even though I considered myself a

Christian, I performed the initiation ceremony many times without questioning it.

I met a young man recently who used to teach Transcendental Meditation. After receiving Christ as his Savior, he tried to continue teaching TM only to find that during the initiation ceremony one day, he physically could not bend his knees before the altar of Guru Dev. He received this as a warning from God and since that time has dropped the practice of TM altogether. He is now a full-time Christian worker.

The fact that TM is a religious practice has implications for the Christian and the non-Christian alike. For the non-Christian or the religiously disinterested, the practice of TM may eventually involve him, whether he recognizes it or not, in a set of experiences and beliefs that center around a concept of God and of the universe that is Hindu. For the Christian, the practice of TM is absolutely forbidden to him by Scripture, for the Biblical revelation is that of a God who will not permit His children to worship other gods. As He says,

> I am the Lord your God, who brought you out of the land of Egypt, out of the house of slavery. You shall have no other gods before Me. You shall not make for yourself an idol, or any likeness of what is in heaven above or on the earth beneath or in the water under the earth. You shall not worship them or serve them; for I, the Lord your God am a jealous God, visiting the iniquity of the fathers on the children, and on the third and the fourth generations of those who hate Me, but showing lovingkindness to thousands, to those who love Me and keep My commandments (Deut. 5:6-10, NASB).

The follow-up lectures after initiation take place during the evenings of the next three consecutive days.

51

By this time, most people have begun to experience some of the effects of meditation.

Every meeting starts with a group meditation. Then the teacher usually asks people if they had any difficulties in meditation or have any questions about the practice. The instructor spends some time discussing the practical benefits of TM in everyday life and how to fit TM into one's daily schedule. Questionnaire sheets are passed out at the beginning and collected at the end of each of the three follow-up lectures. The next day's workshop deals with the mechanics of TM and "stress release" in more detail, and there is a question-and-answer period. The vision of the ultimate goal of meditation is not revealed until the evening of the third workshop. By now many are enjoying greater relaxation and pleasant feelings. It is only at this point that the spiritual aspects of Cosmic-consciousness are outlined briefly and Maharishi's "World Plan" leading to the "Age of Enlightenment" is envisioned as the future outcome of a meditating populace. TM is described as that one thing that will unite all men of all faiths and walks of life everywhere. Thus TM is finally presented as the means of peace and unity (a kind of salvation) for the entire world. Though much is still concealed from the new meditator, enough is revealed to appeal to his spiritual longings for personal and social salvation—the traditional goals of religious teachings of all kinds.

QUESTION: What basic alterations of consciousness are supposed to be caused by TM?

ANSWER: Maharishi describes seven different states of consciousness ranging from the lowest—dreamless sleep, to the highest—Unity-consciousness. Each shift in the state of consciousness is reported to be accompanied by various physiological changes that objectively distinguish one state from another. Early research on the physiological effects of TM was done by Robert Keith Wallace who is now president of Maharishi International University (MIU). His pioneer research on TM was published in *Science* magazine for March 27, 1970. He reported that during TM, oxygen consumption and heart rate decreased, galvanic skin resistance increased, and alpha brain wave production increased. The meditative, or "Transcendental," state is supposed to be distinguished also from sleeping, dreaming, and other altered states such as hypnosis. This state is claimed to be a fourth major state of consciousness along with sleeping, dreaming, and waking. Because the level of metabolism during TM is lower than during sleep, it is claimed to be more restful than sleep. Not all researchers, however, have been able to duplicate all of these results on meditating subjects.

The first four major states of consciousness postulated by Maharishi, then, are: sleeping, dreaming, waking, and Transcendental-consciousness. The other states of consciousness that gradually and cumulatively arise as a result of the twice-daily routine of TM have been called by Maharishi: Cosmic-consciousness, God-consciousness, and Unity-consciousness or Unity.

With the continual swing between the altered or "transcendental" state and normal activity, a time eventually arrives when both transcendental awareness and normal activity exist simultaneously. Maharishi calls this state of divided awareness "Cosmic-consciousness." Once finally gained, it is supposed to be permanent and is maintained whether the meditator is awake, asleep, or dreaming.

The cosmically conscious person, Maharishi says,

experiences his identity as unchanging, eternal, but separate from activity. Those lacking such "enlightenment" are thought to be living in bondage to illusion. Maharishi writes:

> It is a mistake to understand that "I" do this, "I" experience this and "I" know this. All this is basically untrue. The "I," in its essential nature, is uncreated; it belongs to the field of the Absolute. Whereas action, its fruits and the relationship between the doer and his action belong to the relative field, to the field of the three gunas [that is, the forces of nature]. Therefore all action is performed by the three gunas born of nature.[6]

Maharishi says that Cosmic-consciousness is merely the normal condition of the nervous system. The absence of it is the abnormal state. He insists that it is not anything strange. For the meditator, nevertheless, the advent of Cosmic-consciousness is often frightening because of the strange split between self and action. Therefore, a teacher who is already in an "advanced" state of consciousness is given to the student at this point to reassure him with comforting or convenient explanations of the distress he is having.

The next level of consciousness following Cosmic-consciousness is God-consciousness (glorified or refined Cosmic-consciousness, according to more recent terminology). Devotion to "God," of which a person becomes truly capable only in Cosmic-consciousness, is the means to God-consciousness. The heart begins to close the separation between self and activity experienced in Cosmic-consciousness. According to Maharishi's commentary *On the Bhagavad-Gita,* the transition to God-consciousness is brought about by a mental activity of ultimate refinement, devotion to God.[7]

After living in God-consciousness for some time, perception is said to become even more refined so that the finest level of the relative and the Absolute are experienced together. This development is called Unity-consciousness. The person in Unity sees the Absolute and the relative aspects of life ("God" and the world) as one. The distinction between the Supreme Being—God—and the creation is thus denied on the basis of the altered perception of the world that arises from continued practice of TM. This view is diametrically opposed to the Biblical revelation of God as entirely distinct from His creation. Evaluation of this theological viewpoint will be made in chapter 5. It should be understood, however, that a completely subjective view of the world that must be induced by years of disciplined practice of meditation is taken by Maharishi as the absolute standard of truth about reality.

Speaking from personal observation, I no longer believe that the state of Cosmic-consciousness or any of the other effects of TM need be permanent. I recall the first time that it was announced at a group meditation meeting that the state of Cosmic-consciousness was permanent. Several people there expressed alarm at the implication of being permanently locked into an altered state of consciousness. Toward the end of my five years of meditating, I was experiencing "flashes" of "CC" (Cosmic-consciousness) and the experiences were sometimes striking.

For instance, during the night a part of me would be awake even though my body was sound asleep. My "third eye" would be having visions in vivid, beautiful colors, much like an LSD trip. This phenomenon of consciousness during sleep is reported by Maharishi as being a sign of the approach of Cosmic-consciousness. Once, while in this state, I felt a spirit resting on my stomach while I was lying on my back. Immediately I felt and saw a luminous part of my hand slip out of its denser fleshly covering. I probably would have come entirely out of my body if I hadn't sensed a danger in it. Now that I think about it, if I had left, perhaps someone else would have come in. Other experiences happened, such as ESP. Almost every day, toward the end of my five years of meditating, when I would think of somebody, within a half hour or so that person would walk by. Once at a retreat when I was sitting at the dinner table, I saw in my mind's eye a friend of mine coming up behind me. Quickly I turned around, and saw that person actually walking up behind me. These experiences happened so frequently that they became almost commonplace.

Nevertheless, when I received Jesus Christ into my life, the effects of my meditative experiences were wiped out, washed completely away. The Lord showed me by my experience just how impermanent states of mind can be. And I know several meditators who had achieved Cosmic-consciousness who "came down" from that kind of awareness when they came to Jesus in repentance and were born again. They received a new and different awareness; they testify that they now have a conscious communion with the personal Father and the Lord Jesus Christ through the Holy Spirit. Exchanging Cosmic-consciousness for salvation reminds me of the parable Jesus taught about how the kingdom of heaven is like a man who, seeking beautiful pearls, finds one pearl of great price, and goes and sells all that he has that he may buy it (Matt. 13:45-46). Although I experienced ESP, consciousness during sleep, clairvoyance, and restful awareness the TM way, I now see that they were all part of a deception that leads a person away from God and into the depths of the self.

QUESTION: What are the advanced practices and techniques of TM?

ANSWER: There are several things meditators can do to speed up their "progress" into Cosmic-consciousness and beyond.

TM offers weekend retreats, usually in a quiet rural setting, where for a certain fee one can practice more meditations than the usual amount and receive more teachings on TM. There is also an opportunity to discuss personal experiences and special problems that relate to the practice. A demonstration is also given on how to practice hatha yoga *asanas*, which are a series of physical stretching exercises that last for about eight to ten minutes. These are done before and after meditating at these retreats to provide a balance of rest and activity. They also make a person feel more relaxed, which facilitates meditation, and they release stress. Meditators are encouraged to practice these *asanas* every day, but especially at retreats. There are three sets of yoga *asanas*. The first set is very basic and takes about a year to master. The second and the third are a little more difficult. The *asanas* are also taught by an instructor at the TM center to anyone who wants them.

Another technique meditators practice to facilitate relaxation in TM is *pranayama*, a yogic breathing technique. As one breathes in and out in a regular easy fashion, alternately one side of the nasal passage and then the other is blocked by pressing a finger or a thumb on either side of the nose. This is done after the *asanas* for about five minutes. Many people continue to practice *pranayamas* daily before they meditate, whether or not they are at a retreat. *Asanas* and *pranayama* breathing exercises are considered sufficient means in themselves to bring a person to a state of "enlightenment," but using these alone requires more time to reach this goal.

The alternation of *asanas, pranayama,* and meditation, is called "rounding." When I was in TM we were allowed to meditate almost as many times during a weekend retreat as we could, although about five or six times was recommended. Recently, however, because there have been unpleasant, stressful reactions to extended meditation, the number of "rounds" have been cut down to three or four.

To become a teacher of TM, I had to attend a six-week course at Humboldt State College and a three-month teacher-training course in Fiuggi, Italy. At Fiuggi there were approximately six weeks of "rounding" and six weeks of instruction on the Hindu philosophy underlying TM and on the knowledge of the *puja* and the mantras. During the intensive meditation period, some people "rounded" as much as twenty hours a day. I did between ten and twelve hours of "rounding" daily. Again, I would guess that they have cut down the time because of bad reactions. After each day of "rounding," Maharishi would give a lecture in the evening. At one of these lectures I remember seeing a person leaning against a post who looked very spaced out. His eyes were all glassy and staring straight ahead without blinking. I remember noticing his extreme passivity and blank expression, and wondering if he was really quite all there. After many hours of "rounding" I felt, and I'm sure looked, very strange also.

After one has meditated for a year and a half, he

is eligible for an advanced technique. In my case, I received another mantra personally from Maharishi. We were all gathered in a big room, and Maharishi kept us waiting hours beyond the time he had said he would be there. Finally, we had to leave and come back the next day because Maharishi never showed up. There were rumors that his failure to show up that night had cosmic significance. Others said we would appreciate our technique so much more because we had to wait for it. Every year and a half, one can receive another advanced technique. They are said to aid in the development of the heart. Whereas Cosmic-consciousness is described as the full expansion of the mind, God-consciousness is said to be the full development of the heart. One can begin developing devotion through an advanced technique before attaining the level of Cosmic-consciousness, it is claimed. In fact, some people report symptoms or "flashes" of God-consciousness even before Cosmic-consciousness. Likewise, one can have experiences of Cosmic-consciousness ("CC") before he is actually at the level of "CC." I was having experiences of Cosmic-consciousness but I was not in "CC." One of the symptoms of "CC" that I experienced is being conscious during sleep.

The advanced techniques are given out by Maharishi at teacher-training courses or by people he has assigned who make regular tours of the TM centers in the United States and the world for this purpose.

Meditators are encouraged to participate in a continuous program of instruction available without charge at all centers throughout the world. This program includes "checking" and advanced lectures. Checking is a weekly follow-up for the first month and a monthly checkup for the first year, in which a simple, mechanical procedure is employed to insure that the meditator is meditating correctly. Advanced lectures include the showing of films and video tapes of Maharishi. They also provide group meditations, social interaction, and discussions on the more advanced aspects of meditation and experiences in TM.

The checking procedure is given to all who want it by a checker who has memorized the procedure by rote. The checker can respond with computerlike accuracy to any number of possible questions or difficulties with a prepared explanation. The one being checked is not usually aware of the memorized nature of the checking procedure at first. Later he begins to notice that they all sound alike. Many checkers and teachers of TM begin to use the same mannerisms and lilt to their voice as Maharishi. This, plus the impersonality of the checking procedure, is a subject of many jokes among meditators.

After having gone through the memorized procedure, the checker sits with the meditator for about five minutes of meditation. He then leaves the room for approximately fifteen minutes, after which he returns and the meditator is allowed to ask questions. Usually, meditations that are checked are smooth and easy and quite deep.

The SCI (Science of Creative Intelligence) course is a series of thirty-three video-taped lectures by Maharishi on the Hindu philosophy behind TM, and it goes into this in depth. Once a person passes this course, he is eligible to teach it wherever he can. Some are teaching SCI in high schools and colleges as an accredited course. For the most part, I found the SCI course very dry and repetitive. The philosophy is very abstract and hard to grasp. The majority of those who take the SCI course do not go on to teach it, because the SCI course has not been adopted widely enough at the high school level to employ all these trained teachers of SCI. They are available, however, as SCI and TM advance into more schools.

QUESTION: Do meditators change their ideas about God and reality as a result of meditation?

ANSWER: Back in the late 60s, both the Spiritual Regeneration Movement (SRM) and the Student's International Meditation Society (SIMS) put more emphasis on the religious philosophy of TM than they do now. When I began the technique in 1967, SIMS was promoting TM as a five-year plan to reach Bliss-consciousness. Later, the length of time required to reach enlightenment was extended and the "higher" states of consciousness were not discussed until after a person had signed up, paid the fee, and received three days of meditation and checking. This toning down of the spiritual implications of TM has enabled TM to be taught in some public school systems in the United States, but the religious aspect of TM has become the focal point of controversy.

Maharishi, it seems, has decided to tailor the promotion of TM according to his shrewd estimate of the attitudes of modern Western man. Given the predominance of practical materialism today, Maharishi is not promoting TM on the basis of the traditional Hindu goal of spiritual perfection in God-consciousness. He writes that

> ... not in the name of God-Realization can we call a man to meditate in the world of today, but in the name of enjoying the world better, sleeping well at night, being wide awake during the day. If something makes the practical life of man better from day to day, then everyone is for it. ... Very few souls are

61

there in the world today who would go for God alone
. . . the message of a better life in the faith of God,
all that does not satisfy the scientific mind of the jet
age.[8]

Maharishi's expediency in promoting TM is thorough-
going; he trims the presentation of TM to the temper
of the times.

Even when I was still teaching TM, this technologi-
cal approach to TM seemed deceptive to me because
it was leading many people who were only interested
in quitting their smoking habit or in relaxing body
and mind into a mind-altering spiritual practice they
had not bargained for. A typical person would begin
meditation for some of the practical benefits claimed,
find the meditation relaxing and pleasant, and thus
become more open to further spiritual involvement.
When I was in TM, I naively assumed that any spiritual involvement was better than none and this,
therefore, justified getting people into TM by hook
or by crook. Because I believed that "All is One,"
I did not consider the possibility of spiritual counter-
feit and deception.

As an example of the effects of TM on a person's
ideas about God, consider my own case. Just prior to
taking up TM, and following a long period of dis-
affection toward Christianity, I was again seeking the
Lord with renewed interest. I was even reading my
Bible. But as I got deeper into TM, I lost all desire
for personal prayer and Bible reading. My concept of
God as a Person and of Jesus Christ as mediator between man and God gradually changed during the
years I was involved with TM to accommodate the
Hindu concept of God as impersonal. My prior experience with mind-altering drugs also encouraged my
thought in that direction.

Another effect of the practice of TM is the substitution of subjective experience for objective evidence as the standard for truth about reality. In TM, the mind is regularly emptied of thought. Progressively the meditator comes to rely on his subjective feelings and particularly on his experience of meditation as the only standard of reality, rather than upon conclusions based on external standards such as the Bible.

Because science and technology seem to have caused as many problems as they have solved and because they do not provide a satisfying answer to the question of the meaning of life, many people are open to mysticism as the means to knowing the truth. But mysticism involves a negation of the mind, and Christian faith rejects this negation of the rational intellect. In contrast with Eastern mysticism, of which TM is finally a variety, Christianity affirms the importance of the mind as the means for receiving revelation from God through His Word, the Bible. To be sure, the illumination of the Scriptures by the Holy Spirit is necessary for them to be understood, but this does not require either a denial of the full reality of the material creation or a rejection of rationality itself, as does Eastern mysticism.

Therefore, Christian faith is both reasonable and rich in genuine spiritual experience in accordance with God's revelation in Scripture. For the Christian, the Bible is a firm guideline and a protection against false teaching and deceptive experience. The Bible has been opened to my understanding through the illumination of the Holy Spirit and I no longer accept a spiritual experience as being of God without the confirmation of the Word of God.

Everything I was seeking in TM has been more than fulfilled by my Christian experience. I have been completely satisfied without having to abandon my mind. The quality of my spiritual experience has changed from altered awareness to being alive here and now to the God who exists independently of myself.

QUESTION: How did you become a teacher of TM, and why did you finally give it up?

ANSWER:

> Blessed be the God and Father of our Lord Jesus Christ, who hath blessed us with all spiritual blessings in heavenly places in Christ: according as he hath chosen us in him before the foundation of the world, that we should be holy and without blame before him in love, having predestinated us unto the adoption of children by Jesus Christ to himself, according to the good pleasure of his will. (Eph. 1:3-5)

First allow me to give you a brief description of how I became involved in a spiritual search to find the truth about reality and the meaning of life. Even as a child, I was often preoccupied with questions such as: Who am I? Why am I here? Where am I going? I believe that my father's death when I was only five made me perhaps more aware than others of the finitude and preciousness of human life, and the possibility of a life beyond death.

When I was seven years old I discovered the love and grace of Jesus Christ when listening to a radio broadcast of the gospel story. I heard the Spirit of God speak through the actor who was taking the part of Jesus. Convinced that Jesus was God, I hid this knowledge in my heart until four years later. God's servants came to babysit and help out at our house frequently. They would witness to me about Christ's saving power. One of them took me to a youth meeting at a Pentecostal church. I went forward at the altar call and openly received Jesus as my Savior.

At times I experienced a sense of the presence of God when talking with the babysitter, reading a good spiritual book, or thinking about the Lord; but my commitment was not strong enough to overcome the worldly temptations at that time. The pressures from my friends to be popular and the lack of any reality of God in my experience of churchgoing, plus my own rebellious and inquisitive nature (as well as God-given talent), led me exclusively into the arts as a means of expressing and experiencing something higher. I started writing poetry at the age of thirteen, some of which I believe was inspired by the Lord whom I had invited into my life. Here is the first poem I wrote:

> *What strange patterns*
> *The moon plays upon the water,*
> *Like a fisherman's net*
> *Cast across the sea.*
> *It dances so joyously.*
> *In the soft moonlight.*
> *But yet,*
> *There is something mournful*
> *Hidden in the depths:*
> *Of fishermen and sailors*
> *And untold adventurers*
> *Who now lie in solitude,*
> *Buried beneath*
> *That moonlit face.*

This poem strongly suggests an awareness I then had of a distinction between the light and the darkness, good and evil, life and death. There is a hint of the grief of God for a people who have wandered their own way and rejected the path of life.

When I reached my late teens, I became interested in existentialism. *The Stranger* by Camus was one of my favorite books. I went to Lawrence College in Appleton, Wisconsin, because it had high academic standards and yet reasonable admissions requirements. Another reason I went to Appleton was my growing feeling that the world was on the brink of a third world war, and I did not want to be near any big cities. But for me, Appleton was too dull and conservative and I was considered pretty far-out with my manner of dress and my tastes in literature. From existentialism I moved into Eastern philosophy. I devoured anything that had to do with it, starting in a typical fashion with Alan Watts. I also wrote a lot of poetry. But then I came down with mononeucleosis and hepatitis and had to go home.

After switching colleges a couple of times, I finally wound up at U.C. Berkeley with a sigh of relief at the sense of new-found freedom in the air. This was the era of the flower children and the Free Speech Movement. My friends turned me on to pot and LSD and other kinds of hallucinogens, and I took about a dozen psychedelic trips. I read and studied the philosophies of psychedelic gurus Richard Alpert (now Baba Ram Das) and Timothy Leary, which blended nicely with the Eastern mystical path I was already pursuing.

Soon I got involved in rap groups, group-grope marathon encounters, and group therapy, but I was still dissatisfied. Finally, along came Transcendental Meditation in 1967 with Jerry Jarvis speaking placidly and with obvious self-control to a large U.C. audience about the five-year plan to Bliss-consciousness. After waiting in line for seven hours and paying a fee of $35.00, I received my mantra. The very first day I meditated I felt a tangible sensation of peacefulness I had never before experienced, even in my quiet moods. On the third day of meditation, the subject of Cosmic-consciousness was discussed in detail, and I was very enthusiastic about finally unfolding my mental potential and being able to see beyond the material world into Reality.

The first effect of meditation was a calming of my mind and an altering of awareness, which gradually got better than being high on marijuana, so I discontinued smoking pot. As my consciousness changed, I began to become aware of the presence of spirit beings sitting on either side of me when I was meditating. Sometimes at night, uninvited, they would sit on my bed. I thought they were my guardian angels. Once I looked at one of them, and I saw a small dark creature with sharp teeth, who looked more like he wanted to devour me than to bless me. I did not consider the possibility of Satan or his demons at the time but just accepted it as a really weird trip.

After four years of meditating, I decided to learn to be a teacher of TM, so in 1972 I sold my piano, stereo, books, and just about everything I owned, and went to Fiuggi, Italy, where two thousand of us were personally instructed by Maharishi. We spent three months meditating from three to ten hours a day. One night I awoke with a sense of fear and apprehension, because a spirit was putting pressure all over my body and head in an attempt to enter and take possession of my body. I commanded it to leave and resisted it until it left. I did not fully realize the implications of this oppression until later. I began to experience other supernatural sensations—ESP and clairvoyance, telepathy, and the beginnings of astral travel. Maharishi always told us not to delve very deeply into these things but to keep our eyes on the goal (Cosmic-consciousness). I didn't seem to have a choice because these things were happening automatically. And, of course, they were fascinating and unusual.

I attended a few week-long meditation retreats but always at these times I felt lonely because there was no unity or real love among the meditators; every one was so spaced out and cold. This complaint was shared by other meditators. This attitude of detachment was exaggerated by the many hours spent in meditation each day. Once during a meeting a girl started swaying back and forth and screaming, and she finally fell unconscious before anyone moved to help her. I thought she was displaying one of the more unusual symptoms of what TMers refer to as "unstressing" or "normalization of the nervous system." When I saw her distress ignored by myself and many others in this way, I found it alarming.

After I came back from Fiuggi, I took a course in the Science of Creative Intelligence, which presents the Hindu philosophy and tradition behind TM in semi-scientific language so it can be taught in the public schools. This philosophy promoted by Maharishi was alien to me. Even the limited exposure to Christianity I had received as a child was enough to make me feel uncomfortable with it. But this discomfort went deeper than a mere philosophical difference. I sensed in the whole presentation and in the videotaped talks of Maharishi a hypnotic, brainwashing effect that no one else seemed to notice or object to.

It was around this time that I began to ferret out

and gain exposure to other philosophies and occult groups. I was teaching TM at the Berkeley Student's International Meditation Society Center (SIMS) and checking people's meditations, but I was experiencing an increasing disillusionment with the TM movement and a growing sense that there was something fundamentally wrong inside people that TM only seemed to mask.

For instance, TM did not make people more honest. TM was being presented to the public as an innocent, nonreligious technique when in reality it was a heavy spiritual practice. So a person could sign up, pay the fee, and get high meditating for three days before he was even told about the spiritual direction he was taking. I felt an uneasiness over the fact that each person tended to become his/her own standard of morality and of reality. Is everything we experience legitimate? Does anything go? Where was the standard? *Was* there a standard?

I personally knew meditators who had been practicing TM for many years who were getting divorces. If TM increased awareness and love, why couldn't they make their marriages work? Many times I was surprised at my own growing pride and insensitivity to others even though I felt more calm and confident than ever before. I was becoming, in fact, my own god. I didn't like the direction TM was taking me.

As the months went by I could see more and more that something was missing. We were all supposed to be getting closer to God, but no one, not even those in "God-consciousness," ever praised God or gave Him thanks, or, if they did, it was not something they could share openly.

So, contrary to the rules set down by the TM center for TM teachers, my desire to know the truth and to serve God led me to investigate other philosophies and occult practices while maintaining my twice daily routine of TM. I still would not condescend to go to church or read the Bible. After all, hadn't I already been through that trip? Besides, I was still enjoying myself immensely and getting really high on TM. Psychic occurrences were becoming the norm for me. My art and music were blossoming; I had no reason to doubt the effectiveness of TM. The only thing that still bothered me was this sense that I was becoming the center of my universe; yet I did not know who God really was or how to worship Him. If God was all powerful and all merciful, why couldn't He make Himself known to me; why did I have to climb my way up to Him?

I was beginning to move towards "Cosmic-consciousness." There was creeping into every recess of my being a feeling of oneness, which was like an all-pervading noxious gas choking my mind. The oneness felt good; it made everything look beautiful; it seemed like a mellow attitude to have; but it was numbing my conscience and giving me an enormous spiritual pride.

I looked into Meher Baba and Krishna Consciousness. I spent about two weeks chanting Hare Krishna and sitting on campus listening to one of the leaders of the Krishna movement read from the Bhagavad-Gita and expound his particular Hindu philosophy. When I shared with them my TM philosophy (Vedanta), they told me that I was following a deceptive path. TM teaches that ultimately, at the end of one's spiritual journey, one loses his own personal identity and becomes absorbed into the Godhead like a drop of water merging with the ocean. But the Krishnas told me that this was a deceptive teaching. They used an analogy for the relationship of man and God of a green bird landing in a green tree. They may both be the same color and meant for each other, but the bird retains its separate identity. In other words, as the bird does not become the tree, so a man does not become God.

I liked the Krishna devotees' sense of devotion and service. It did seem to me a higher thing to worship God than to "be" God. Love always seems to involve a relationship of some kind. But I could not relate to their god who was a little blue man with a flute. While attending their meetings, I met a young man named John with remarkable psychic powers who also had some knowledge about Jesus. He could, with surprising accuracy, read auras and do psychic readings on people he had never met. At the time, I was interested in developing my own psychic powers, so I asked him to teach me how. He said that we should get a group of friends together and he would teach us some things.

Every night for about a week John held a group meditation. He raised our energy levels with the power of his mind. We did a series of chants, first calling on names of friends that we knew, then invoking the names of various deities and religious masters such as Rama, Krishna, and Buddha. We would connect into the psychic field of each one, and get very high in a different way with each one.

Finally, he said, "These and other chants and exercises will make you blissful, but there is one that will make you clean. It is the only name that will give you righteousness and peace. He can set you free from the material world because He's beyond it. Let's all join hands and vocally call on the name of Jesus. For in the Bible, it says, 'Those who call on the name of the Lord shall be saved.' There is great power in the spoken word."

71

It was really hard to call on the name above all names. Every other name was easy, but not the name of Jesus. We would call "Jesus," "Jesus, cleanse me," or "Jesus, fill me," over and over. It was embarrassing, difficult, and strangely unsettling. John said that this was caused by two things: first, from guilt trips and false images of Christianity that had been laid upon us by society; and second, because the name of Jesus is so pure, so holy, and so powerful that He starts to stir up layers of impurity in our lives and begins to clean them out.

For six days I spent an extra fifteen minutes in addition to my TM just calling on Jesus. It was audible and not like a mantra, in that I actually tried to reach out to Him personally. Each day I felt *worse*, not better. I was surprised at the anger and hostility in me that this name seemed to be surfacing. I felt like I was on unstable ground for the first time in years. Where was my TM bliss?

I almost ceased calling on Jesus' name, because I didn't like what I was seeing in myself. At the same time, I had a lot of respect for the power of that name, and attributed my misery to its cleansing effect and assumed that once the garbage was out, I'd feel better.

One night as I was calling on the Lord with John, a sense of holiness filled the room, and a visible heavenly light descended upon me from above, as if the heavens had opened, and it seemed to fill me inwardly to overflowing. There was a peace and fulfillment in my heart. I knew that I had reached the end of my search for God. I was introduced into a spiritual realm that was as different from what I had experienced in TM as night from day.

Since becoming a Christian I have encountered the

same kind of spirits I used to experience during TM. The Lord has given me discernment, and I now see that they are demons. Before I became a Christian, these demons seldom bothered me and I even mistook them for guardian angels at times; but after I was born again through Christ, they became very hostile and tried to overpower me on several occasions. They always had to leave when I commanded them to go in the name of Jesus. The Bible says Satan often comes as an angel of light to deceive people. Many believe that the intensity of Satan's deception is to be greatest in the last days before Christ's bodily return to earth; I believe these are the last days.

The Lord has opened my eyes not only to His glory and the beauties of His creation, but also to the spiritual battle being waged between the heavenly kingdom of God and the holy angels, and Satan and his fallen angels. The object of the conflict is your soul. You must choose to serve on one side or the other.

I would sum up my reason for getting into TM as being the result of my spiritual search to fulfill the human need to experience something beyond the senses and matter. TM temporarily satisfied that need, but it finally proved to be a dead end. It involved me in the deception of presenting TM as a non-religious technique when it is really a thinly-disguised Hindu practice, and it didn't fulfill the need for a personal relationship with God. On the contrary, it drew me further away from the Lord by involving me in spiritual exercises and experiences that are contrary to the Word of God. Therefore, I got out of TM for the same reason I got into it; I was seeking the truth about reality, and I have found that truth in the Lord Jesus Christ. His revelation was for me unexpected but totally fulfilling.

Notes

1. Sir John Woodruffe, *The Garland of Letters* (Ganesh: Madras, India, 1922), p. 261.
2. Maharishi Mahesh Yogi, *Meditations of Maharishi Mahesh Yogi* (New York: Bantam Books, 1968), p. 18.
3. Jack Forem, *Transcendental Meditation: Maharishi Mahesh Yogi and the Science of Creative Intelligence* (New York: Dutton, 1973), p. 40.
4. Anonymous, "The Holy Tradition" (No publication data), p. 6.
5. Ibid., pp. 4-5.
6. Maharishi, *On the Bhagavad-Gita: A New Translation and Commentary,* chapters 1-6 (Baltimore: Penguin Books, 1967), p. 352.
7. Ibid., pp. 309, 313.
8. Maharishi, *Meditations,* pp. 168-169.

CHAPTER THREE

Transcendental Meditation: The Scientific View

by David Haddon

QUESTION: Are the WPEC claims for the beneficial physical and psychological effects of TM scientifically established?

ANSWER: The World Plan Executive Council (WPEC) publishes a promotional booklet entitled *Fundamentals of Progress* presenting scientific research on TM in the form of charts and graphs with commentary. On the basis of these selected studies, WPEC claims that a wide variety of physical and psychological benefits spring from TM. Physical benefits claimed include rest and relaxation; increased efficiency of heart and lungs; faster reaction time; improved coordination; strengthened immune system; and relief from stress-related psychosomatic illnesses such as high blood pressure, allergy, asthma, and insomnia. Psychological benefits claimed include greater calmness and stability, improved perception, increased intelligence, memory, and learning ability, improved psychological health, and improved interpersonal relationships.

A truly scientific viewpoint must acknowledge the limitations of the studies upon which such claims have been based. Dr. Peter Fenwick, a British neurophysiologist basically sympathetic to TM but conscious also of what constitutes scientific proof, provided a scientific perspective on TM studies to *London Times* readers when he wrote:

> All these studies need to be looked upon with reservations. Few include adequate control groups and none that I am aware of have yet used a blind control procedure where neither the subject nor observer is aware of the treatment given or the aims of the experiment. Until this sort of study is carried out in meditating groups it is almost impossible to draw any conclusion.
>
> Psychological results are capable of being influenced by many non-specific factors, and those of us in psychiatry are aware of the large numbers of treatments which have been hailed as the panacea in their time, but which have later been shown to have their effects entirely in a non-specific way.[1]

Fenwick does consider that TM has been scientifically established as a relaxation technique, but that is about all.

Among the "non-specific" factors Fenwick refers to that may cause the benefits attributed to TM are the "placebo effect," which comes from the inevitable suggestion that TM will be beneficial (the motivation to self-improvement typical of beginning any therapeutic activity), and the commitment to TM as a way of life.

Two researchers on TM writing in April 1974 *Psychology Today* criticized WPEC's use of scientific data to present TM in the best-possible light. Leon Otis, a Department Director at Stanford Research Institute (SRI), cited WPEC's "misuse of data."[2] And Gary Schwartz, a Harvard psychology professor not unsympathetic to TM, nevertheless cautions that "we should remain wary of the claims and selective use of scientific data by well-meaning but scientifically unsophisticated practitioners."[3]

Otis also noted that his researchers did not reproduce the same striking changes in metabolic levels during meditation that Wallace had recorded in his physiological study that opened the door to extensive research on TM. Otis writes:

> My associates, Jerome Lukas and Arthur Vassiliadis, who conducted the physiological studies, believe that TM has little effect on heart rate or blood pressure, and that the simple act of resting every day over a three-month period may produce more alpha waves than meditation.[4]

Similarly, Schwartz reported that his research at Harvard failed to reproduce the large increases in skin-resistance (a measure of anxiety level) that Wallace reported. Schwartz goes so far as to suggest that Wallace's work may have been in error.

To both Schwartz at Harvard and the SRI researchers, it came to appear that many of the effects associated with TM by preliminary research may actually come from causes other than the meditation itself. Dr. Otis's interviews with the meditators in the SRI study led him to conclude that "expectancy plays a critical role in whatever benefits accrue to an individual from practicing TM, and that an important contributor may also be the mere practice of sitting quietly in a relaxed posture."[5] Expectancy, it may be noted in passing, is a synonym for faith.

Another researcher who has come to similar conclusions about the role of expectations in the beneficial effects of TM is Dr. Jonathan Smith, Professor of Psychology at Roosevelt University in Chicago. For his doctoral dissertation at the University of Michigan, he investigated the effects of TM in relieving anxiety and associated psychosomatic symptoms. Since it is impossible to escape expectation of improvement in mental health in those taught TM, Smith devised a control procedure called PSI (Periodic Somatic Inactivity), which was merely to sit with eyes closed daily for a certain period of time. Expectations of benefit similar to those fostered in TM were built by presenting PSI introductory lectures, formal PSI instruction, and follow-up PSI meetings on the TM model. The results of this experiment "show six months of TM to be no more effective in reducing anxiety than six months of PSI. . . ."[6] He concluded that TM, as it is presented, has psychotherapeutic potential, but that its effectiveness may come not from the meditation but from "(a) expectation of relief and (b) the regular practice of sitting quietly."[7]

Smith makes another cogent criticism that applies to many studies comparing groups of people who start meditation with a control group of people who have no particular motivation to self-improvement. He writes of the meditators in such studies that "such motivated subjects may be ripe for growth and may display reductions in pathology regardless of what they choose to do."[8] Because those who start meditation have a motivation to self-improvement and an expectation to improve, they are not comparable to a control group with neither motivation to improve nor expectation of improvement. These considerations would seem to apply equally to other physical and psychological benefits claimed in the *Fundamentals of Progress* booklet on the basis of comparisons between meditators and unmotivated control groups.

The use of TM as a psychotherapeutic technique at the Institute for Living in Hartford, Connecticut, has been widely publicized as a demonstration of the value of TM in psychotherapy. Dr. Bernard C. Glueck, director of research there, has appeared on television with Maharishi himself to testify to the value of TM to the patients at the Institute. *The Hartford Courant* (October 3, 1975), however, has reported that TM has been dropped as a treatment at the Institute. A first-page story entitled "Disagreement at Institute" quotes Psychiatrist-in-chief John Donnelly as saying with regard to TM therapy that "our findings did not indicate any significant difference in the treatment of psychiatric disorders." The article continues:

> Donnelly said Thursday that since TM depends on teaching its users a secret word or "mantra," it violates the ethics of medicine and cannot be tested scientifically. Without proof of its effectiveness, he said, it cannot be considered a treatment. . . . Donnelly said at the Institute that TM benefits are found in "those who believe in it."

For these reasons the use of TM at the Institute has been discontinued and patients are not permitted to seek instruction at the local TM center on their own because "it would interfere with their hospital treatment."[9] Apparently the psychotherapeutic value of TM remains controversial among psychiatrists.

From the studies and analysis of researchers such as Smith, Schwartz, and Otis described above, it should be apparent that the supposed beneficial effects of TM have not been scientifically established. The work of Leon Otis and of Jonathan Smith in particular calls into question the claim that the practice of TM is responsible for the benefits observed. Both of these researchers have concluded that simply sitting quietly with eyes closed along with the expectancy raised by the way TM is presented may be the basis for much of the apparent effect of TM on psychosomatic and psychopathic conditions. Other factors possibly affecting the results suggested by these researchers are the motivation to self-improvement typical of the beginning meditator and the commitment to TM as a way of life typical to the TM teacher.

It does seem that TM lowers metabolism, relaxes the body, and may calm the mind during its practice. As for most of the rest of its claimed benefits, it is not yet possible to affirm or deny with any certainty whether TM directly causes them. There is reason to doubt that TM itself is the cause in many cases. The factors of positive expectations aroused by the suggestions from TM teachers, the sitting quietly every day, the motivation of self-improvement, and commitment to TM as a way of life are other possible causes of benefits observed. Certainly it has not been scientifically established that TM causes the host of physical and psychological benefits attributed to it by Maharishi and WPEC.

The unwarranted claim that these benefits have been scientifically established, however, is evidence of the truth of one of Maharishi's statements about TM. Maharishi wrote that "the practice of transcendental meditation ... brings faith. ..."[10] The faith in

TM that arises from its practice has caused WPEC officials to make claims for TM that go beyond what has actually been proven. It is a misplaced faith which so undermines objectivity that the distinction between what is scientifically established and that which remains to be proved is lost. WPEC's *Fundamentals of Progress* booklet is an expression of just such a faith. This is the kind of faith to which, as Maharishi promises, TM leads.

QUESTION: How scientific is the Science of Creative Intelligence?

ANSWER: According to an MIU leaflet, "Science of Creative Intelligence: A Short Introduction," "A science is taken to be a systematic investigation by means of repeatable experiment to gain useful and testable knowledge." From this definition's reference to "repeatable experiment," it appears that MIU wishes to associate SCI with empirical science and its public prestige. The practice of this "science," however, is diametrically opposed to that of empirical science in that "it is a process of direct experience and not of intellectual analysis." By "direct experience" is meant the subjective experience of meditation in TM. Thus it is apparent that SCI is not scientific in the commonly understood and prestigious sense relating to empirical science.

Actually SCI is a religious philosophy presented in quasi-scientific language, as readily appears in its definition. Another MIU brochure defines SCI as

> the study of the nature, origin, range, growth and application of creative intelligence. This science arose from the major discovery that there exists throughout creation and in every human being an *inexhausti-*

81

> *ble source of intelligence, energy and happiness ...*
> (emphasis added).

How was this "major discovery" of the "inexhaustible source" of creation made? Certainly not on the basis of empirical science, because the inherently limited data of such studies cannot establish the nature nor even the existence of an "inexhaustible" or infinite "source." Philosophy and religion deal with the infinite source of creation in view in SCI. Since the approach of SCI is theoretical, it is best described as a religious philosophy.

The basis of the "major discovery" from which SCI arose was not empirical science nor even the "direct experience" of a host of meditators, but rather the Hindu scriptures, the Upanishads, the Vedas, and the Bhagavad-Gita. Jack Forem, a TM area coordinator, makes this clear in his book, *Transcendental Meditation: Maharishi Mahesh Yogi and the Science of Creative Intelligence*, when he writes:

> Everything in the relative field of life ... is nothing but various manifestations of Being, which is absolute and unchanging. There is a famous saying in the *Upanishads* which expresses this fact: "I am That, Thou art That, all this is nothing but That."[11]

The particular philosophical understanding of these scriptures, from which SCI comes, is that of the Shankara tradition of Hinduism in which Maharishi was trained. This claim can be demonstrated by comparing the premises of Shankara's Hindu philosophy with descriptions of SCI by Forem from his "MIU Press" text on TM and SCI.

Two fundamental points of Shankara's philosophy are:

1. The underlying unity of all existence as Brahman or Being (i.e., "All is One").[12]
2. The identity of the self of man with the Self of the universe (the identity of *jiva* with *Atman/Brahman* in Maharishi's formulation.[13]

Compare the following statements from Forem's book:

1. The science of creative intelligence asserts . . . that underlying the myriad . . . forms and phenomena of life is . . . an unbounded field of pure creative intelligence. . . ."[14] All fields of life spring from one source: Being, the underlying, unbounded ocean of creative intelligence and energy. . . .[15]

2. The science of creative intelligence intellectually locates the "I," the self, and defines it as a field of pure consciousness, a field of energy and creative intelligence, the source of all thought.[16]

The identity of the two pairs of statements is apparent. The main difference is just the substitution of synonyms like "pure consciousness," "source of all thought," and "creative intelligence" for another set of synonyms: "Self," "Being," and "Brahman."

The Science of Creative Intelligence, then, is not scientific in the common understanding of the word. It is, rather, a religious philosophy: the Hindu monism of the tradition of Shankara as interpreted by Maharishi.

QUESTION: Has TM been scientifically established as an effective drug-abuse control measure?

ANSWER: TM has been highly touted as a drug-abuse control measure since a statistical correlation between persistence in practicing TM and self-reported reduction in drug abuse was obtained by Wallace and Benson from the replies to questionnaires by 1,862 meditators training to become TM teachers.[17] On the basis of such reports (and the testimonials of meditators who stop drug abuse) and because of the severity of the drug-abuse problem in American society, government officials and even military leaders have promoted TM among students, soldiers, and young people generally. The Illinois Assembly Resolution (HR 677) encouraging the adoption of TM and SCI in Illinois schools, for example, states that "Transcendental Meditation offers an alternative to drug abuse and studies indicate that it shows promise of being *the most positive and effective drug prevention program being presented in the world today*" (SIMS reprint; emphasis added).

Despite the impression created by the Benson and Wallace study cited above and the acceptance given TM as a drug-abuse control measure by various officials, TM has not been scientifically established as a generally applicable drug-abuse control measure. A paper presented to the Kentucky Academy of Science points out that

> . . . one of the advertised inferred advantages of TM is that it may decrease drug or alcohol dependency in users. . . . This tentative conclusion must be viewed with the utmost skepticism for the following reason. Prior to initiation, a user must abstain from (nonprescribed) drugs 15 days. This means that of initiates who were dependent, they must have been much less than highly dependent or addicted prior to initiation. In short, by means of the 15-day abstinence period, a population pre-selection is already taking place against the hard-core dependent abuser, thus leaving the lower dependency user who then becomes a TM initiate. Therefore, subsequent change in de-

pendency following TM cannot be expected for the general drug-user population with any degree of validity.[18]

Harvard psychologist Gary Schwartz writes of the effect of TM on drug use:

> There is a process of self-selection involved here. There are also strong group pressures to conform to the model of the successful meditator, who presumably has transcended drugs. . . . Placebo factors may also be operating. . . . The assertion, in short, that TM cures drug abuse may be true but remains unproven.[19]

Writing on the same subject, Leon Otis of Stanford Research Institute maintains that because

> SIMS keeps no records of people who *quit* TM . . . if we learn that nearly every experienced meditator has given up drugs, that's all we know. We don't know whether most people, when they start meditating, stop abusing drugs; we don't know whether TM itself or some concurrent process is changing their drug habits; and we don't know what other techniques, decisions or changes of circumstances might have done the same thing.[20]

Professor Jonathan Smith of the Department of Psychology at Roosevelt University in Chicago is particularly critical of all research on TM such as the Benson and Wallace study done on the basis of questionnaires sent to meditators. He comments that

> the major weakness of these studies is that they relied on data resembling solicited testimonials. . . . The sample of those who volunteered to participate in meditation research was perhaps *not* representative of the population of those who learned to meditate. We cannot conclude from such studies that the practice of meditation is therapeutic.[21]

Benson himself acknowledged some of the limitations of his and Wallace's initial study and began another study that failed to gain very many student participants, apparently because of lack of motivation on the part of young drug abusers to start and continue TM. In the selected high schools in Michigan and Massachusetts where TM was offered to several thousand students who had answered a questionnaire on their drug-use habits, only thirty-six students became meditators and only six of these persisted in meditation.[22] The obvious conclusion from this significant result would seem to be that TM is a monumental flop at drug-abuse prevention when applied "across the board" to drug users and others not already motivated to avoid drug abuse.

When TM is introduced to a group of drug abusers, then, many refuse to start or fail to continue TM. Of those who continue TM, its effects on their drug use may vary with the strength of their commitment to TM. Researcher Otis comments on the relationship between commitment to TM and reduction of drug abuse that

> a person's depth of motivation and his commitment to TM as a way of life are probably . . . important variables. Consider drugs, for instance. The teacher-trainees who had used drugs indicated that almost all had given them up. But only about half of the randomly polled SIMS group and only about a quarter of the drop-outs had stopped taking drugs.[23]

For drug abusers who start TM and stop drug abuse, a substitution of TM as a way of life for the former way of life is likely. Whenever TM is accepted to the extent that a person wants to devote himself to teaching it, drugs are likely to be given up completely because they are not part of the way of life Maharishi approves among his followers. Possibly, part of the reason for this substitution of life-styles is that the consciousness alteration by TM is preferred to that of drugs, but it is not the only cause operating.

That a scientific researcher (Otis) has noted the tendency of TM to become a way of life for some of those who begin its practice is important because TM is presented as an innocent technique rather than as an alternative way of life. Just as SIMS denies the religious implications of TM, so it also specifically denies that TM involves changing one's way of life. In both cases, there is a violation of simple truthfulness in the presentation of TM. Few, if any, scientists have concerned themselves with this ethical issue, but it is an important consideration in both private and public decisions about the adoption of TM.

To sum up, TM has not been established scientifically as a generally applicable drug-abuse prevention or control measure. Its requirements ordinarily screen out the addicted, and concurrent factors such as suggestion, prior motivation, and social pressure may explain why many meditators stop drug use. None of the studies on drug abuse and TM put forth by the MIU International Center for Scientific Research fully meets these objections. Benson's attempt to run a large-scale study overcoming the scientific deficiencies of the earlier Benson and Wallace study merely demonstrated the ineffectiveness of TM as a general drug-abuse control measure. That TM has a strong potential to become a way of life and that its beneficial effects are dependent on commitment to TM as a way of life have been observed in the course of scientific research on TM.

The use of TM as a general drug-abuse control measure evidently is futile for this purpose, but such programs may well select out those who are open to making a personal commitment to the way of life associated with TM. For public agencies to enlist the aid of religious groups offering a morally sound way of life in combatting moral problems like drug abuse is eminently reasonable and of long use in this country. WPEC and SIMS, however, have disqualified themselves for such public support by operating under false pretenses about TM's tendency to become a way of life as well as about its nature as a religious practice. The way of life associated with TM is not morally sound because of the deception involved in its promotion and teaching.

QUESTION: Have any harmful effects of TM been observed by scientists?

ANSWER: Yes, some harmful effects from the practice of TM have been observed, and other possible harmful effects have been warned against by scientists. In the *Psychology of Transcendental Meditation: A Literature Review*, a Stanford Research Institute report, it is stated that "Otis (1972) found that TM resulted in an increase in drug abuse in some individuals and that approximately 23% of the Humboldt population of regular meditators reported an increase in their antisocial behavior."[24] It should be noted that a large majority of meditators reported reduced drug use and reduced antisocial behavior.

In *Psychology Today*, Leon Otis reported that some people doing TM or a similar experimental technique using a mock mantra suffered from recurrence of psychosomatic symptoms previously under control. Two subjects reciting mock mantras and three doing TM dropped out of the experiment because of the severity of their distress. Their problems included recurrence of a bleeding ulcer, depression requiring psychiatric care, and agitation leading to the loss of a job. Otis comments that "an extremely anxious person who has managed to restrain his anxiety may find that the deep calm of mantra meditation 'liberates' nothing but problems."[25]

Probably the unkindest cut TM has received at the hands of a researcher was based on Harvard psychologist Gary Schwartz's testing of sixteen TM teachers on two standardized measures of creativity. He reported that "surprisingly, the meditators scored no better than the nonmeditators. On some scales, in fact, the meditators did consistently worse. The result was especially interesting because the meditators were trying hard to succeed. On other tests, however, . . . the meditators scored consistently higher than the controls." Schwartz suggests that "too much meditation may interfere with a person's logical . . . processes, or the sort of problem-solving creativity required by the Wallace-Kogan test."[26] Writing in the July 1975 *Psychology Today,* Colin Martindale, a professor of psychology at the University of Maine, cites Schwartz's findings and his own study of creativity to challenge the claim that TM promotes creativity. He states that

> people who practice TM regularly have few spontaneous fluctuations in their skin conductance, but creative people have many. It's possible, then, that all the effort to promote biofeedback gadgets, alpha machines, meditation, transcendental or otherwise, may have the side effect of decreasing our ability to think creatively.[27]

These possibly harmful effects of TM are no more

established scientifically than the beneficial effects, but they are less commonly reported by researchers.

Negative effects from TM, then, have been observed by researchers, but they are never reported by Maharishi's organizations, which strive only to present data favorable to TM. The scientific view, however, requires that all known information be presented. Since the general public has heard only one side of TM—that presented by Maharishi's followers—it is necessary to present some of the negative data here. In conclusion, though a majority of meditators report favorable effects, some meditators report increased antisocial behavior and increased drug use after beginning TM. Because experimental subjects doing TM have suffered from the release of anxieties they were unable to cope with, researchers have cautioned the extremely anxious against TM. The possibility that TM may interfere with logical thought and creativity has also been suggested by researchers. In general, these scientific critics are not opposed to TM as a relaxation technique. They merely point out that TM is not the universal panacea its promoters tend to claim it to be and that its practice poses some hazards.

QUESTION: Can TM or Benson's "Relaxation Response" meditation technique cure high blood pressure?

ANSWER: Harvard Medical School cardiologist Herbert Benson believes, on the basis of his research, that TM and other meditative practices such as the secular technique he has devised can be helpful in reducing excessive blood pressure. He holds that such meditative techniques bring on a restful state he calls the "Relaxation Response." Benson's view of the effect of meditation on high blood pressure is not yet accepted by cardiologists generally. Dr. John Laragh, described by *Time* magazine as "perhaps the leading expert on hypertension in the U.S." said, "I'm not sure that meditating has had any different effect on blood pressure than relaxing and sitting on a couch and reading a book."[28] Dr. Laragh plans a study to determine the effects of meditation on high blood pressure. With disagreement current among such authorities, it is probably wise to withhold judgment on whether one or another form of relaxation is more effective in lowering blood pressure.

Benson's claims for meditation are modest enough in any case when they are closely examined. Though he considers meditation helpful in the control of high blood pressure, he does not consider it to be a cure at all. In discussing an experiment in which the blood pressure of persons with high blood pressure was lowered "from the borderline high blood pressure range to the 'normal range'" after they had practiced TM for several weeks, Benson points out that "the meditation had not *cured* them. The subjects' lower blood pressure readings lasted ony as long as they practiced the Relaxation Response [via TM in this case] regularly. When [seven] ... subjects ... chose to *stop* the regular practice of Transcendental Meditation, their blood pressures returned to their initial hypertensive levels within four weeks."[29]

Benson thinks that the effect of meditation in counteracting activity of the sympathetic nervous system is like that of some drugs used against high blood pressure. In cases of even moderate high blood pressure, however, Benson doubts that meditation can be more than an adjunct to drug therapy. He writes:

It is unlikely that the regular elicitation of the Relaxation Response [by meditation] by itself will prove to be adequate therapy for severe or moderate high blood pressure.[30]

Thus Benson acknowledges the rather great limitations of meditation in treatment of high blood pressure. In his opinion, only in mild cases could it provide a substitute for all medication, and then only under a doctor's supervision. Other medical opinion, as noted above, questions whether meditation is any better in lowering blood pressure than conventional forms of relaxation.

Benson acknowledges, then, that the "Relaxation Response" supposedly caused by TM, the Benson technique, and other meditative practices are not a "cure" but at best an ameliorative in the case of borderline high blood pressure. Its effectiveness is dependent on a lifetime continuance of the practice. Superficially, at least, Benson appears to have cut his technique loose from the religious traditions from which he has drawn it—as Maharishi has not. Therefore it might seem acceptable to a Christian or Jew for whom the idolatrous ritual of the initiation ceremony of TM is an insurmountable objection. But the traditions from which Benson purports to draw his technique are essentially the *mystical* traditions of the major religions. These mystical techniques have psycho-spiritual effects as well as psycho-physiological effects. A common effect of these practices is the onset of unitive mystical experience which readily tends to be interpreted as an experience of the meditator's inner oneness with "God." Another effect of such mystical experience is to make the meditator's inner experience the source of knowledge about God and reality rather than the written revelation of God's Word, the Bible.

Christians who are already experiencing the loving union of sonship with God through the mediation of Christ accept the authority of the Bible as Christ did (Matt. 5:17-19) rather than that of the subjective experience of mysticism. They naturally reject a life-time commitment to a practice tending toward the illusion of union with God unmediated by Jesus Christ.

In conclusion, Benson does not claim that TM or his "Relaxation Response" meditation will cure high blood pressure, because the techniques must be continued indefinitely. Even when so continued, Benson claims only marginal, though significant and beneficial, lowering of blood pressure. The spiritual tendency of Benson's technique, like that of the mystical traditions from which he draws it, is away from the personal Creator to whom we have access only through Jesus Christ.

QUESTION: What are the attitudes of scientists generally toward Maharishi and TM?

ANSWER: The attitudes of scientists toward Maharishi run the gamut from devotion to rejection and contempt. Their attitude toward TM is generally respectful because of the physiological research that seems to indicate that TM alters body metabolism in a way not understood by science. Many, therefore, accept it as another useful relaxation technique. Others credit TM with saving some of their students from drug abuse. Some practice TM themselves. Brian Josephson, the British Nobel prizewinner in physics for 1973, is a typical scientist-meditator. Although he finds TM personally useful, he acknowledges that others may find it useless.

A small group of scientists have become devoted to Maharishi and apparently are convinced that SCI and TM are the keys to the knowledge of reality. Physiologist Robert Keith Wallace, whose doctoral work at UCLA on the physiological effects of TM pioneered the expansion of scientific study of TM and greatly accelerated the acceptance of TM by the academic community, is one such scientist. From his role as a meditating graduate student in physiology, his research has catapulted him into the presidency of Maharishi International University. Another scientist who has been given a university headship in view of his scientific services to Maharishi is physicist Lawrence Domash, who is Chancellor of Maharishi European Research University (MERU). Paul H. Levine, who holds a Ph.D. in theoretical physics from Cal Tech and who has been chief scientist of the Astrophysics Research Corporation in Los Angeles, is another scientist-devotee. In the December 1972 *Phi Delta Kappan,* he wrote for its audience of educators that "creative intelligence may be said to be both the goal and the source of education," thus promoting SCI and TM among a crucial group.[31]

Another scientist who is devoting himself to spreading TM is Walter Koch. From a background in outer space research for the General Motors Research Laboratory, Koch has shifted his attention to inner space vía TM. He now develops large-scale meditation programs for industry and prisons as Associate Director of TM's Institution for Social Rehabilitation. Another academician who speaks well of TM is Professor John Lewis of the Massachusetts Institute of Technology. He has taped lectures for MIU and contends that TM breaks down the mental barriers to learning untouched by conventional education.

Science magazine for March 28, 1975, provides some

less favorable viewpoints on Maharishi, though TM itself is viewed uncritically:

> MIU tries to give the impression that it has the endorsement of great minds in scholarship and science, many of whose names are scattered about the [MIU] catalog. But such is not quite the case. Chemist and Nobel prizewinner Melvin Calvin of the University of California at Berkeley says he addressed one of the SCI symposia, but he considers use of his name in the catalog as coming "perilously close to false advertising." Calvin . . . asserts, "Maharishi's principal business is collecting money from new acolytes. He doesn't know anything about science," but does know that cloaking his dogma in scientific jargon is the only way to gain legitimacy. In the 1960s, says Calvin, Maharishi helped hundreds of students kick drugs—"if it weren't for the rescue job he did around here he'd have absolutely no sympathy from me at all." Mael Melvin, who teaches quantum mechanics at Temple University, used to give lectures at one of the IMS New York centers, but has since disassociated himself from the movement, saying, "Maharishi is flexible in what he considers truth."[32]

Time magazine for October 13, 1975, provides another slightly critical view:

> Anyone who claims exclusivity is immediately suspect," says Psychiatrist Stanley Dean, summing up the chief scientific complaint against TM. "The TM people's claim that theirs is the best of all possible worlds is nonsense. It is a sales gimmick. Meditation has been a way of achieving mental serenity through the ages, and they have no patent on it. TM is an important addition to our medical armamentarium, but it is not exclusive.[33]

Some of these scientists have noticed certain irregularities in the conduct of Maharishi and his organizations in the promotion of TM. Mael Melvin in the *Science* article even raised the key issue of Maharishi's truthfulness. Aside from Dean's criticism of TM's claim to exclusivity, there is little criticism of the claims to various benefits beyond relaxation from the practice of TM. This may be because these scientists were unaware of the inadequacies of experimental design that call into question the causal relation between the practice of TM and many of the reported benefits.

Many scientists are scarcely concerned about the issue of the religious and cultic significance of TM and similar practices. Apparently they are content to evaluate TM itself solely in terms of its physical effects. And evidently they view it from the naïvely materialistic perspective that still pervades the academic-scientific world even where it is not openly avowed. Editorial replies to a letter to the *Journal* of the American Medical Association from a doctor who was refused instruction in TM when he objected to the "religious type ritual" of the initiation ceremony strikingly expose this attitude. The doctor asked whether TM is science or a cult. In reply, Harvard cardiologist and TM researcher Herbert Benson dismissed the religious aspect of the question entirely in one sentence by saying with total relativism, "Whether transcendental meditation is a cult depends on one's own definition of cult."[34] Benson thus refused to waste any time defining terms in matters of religion, but he did go on to affirm in some detail that TM causes a physiological response of relaxation that has therapeutic potential. In another reply to the same letter, *Journal* editor Lester S. King dealt with the religious aspect of the question by encouraging the doctor to disregard his misgivings about the TM ritual (perhaps violating his conscience in the process) for the sake of the possible physical benefits. Doctor King advised:

> Since we are dealing with a practical problem of body control, it is, I believe, wise to accept details of the particular discipline you are pursuing. It is not necessary to accept the ultimate metaphysical postulates, but the discipline that ritual can provide may be quite important for that particular technique. I think we can separate religious convictions from ritual that contributes to self-control. Cut flowers and a white handkerchief would seem a small price to pay for sound sleep and lowered blood pressure, and not inconsistent with religious convictions.[35]

King nicely articulates the conclusion of expediency for the sake of physical benefits. King is probably unaware of the strictly idolatrous nature of the ceremony; but his materialistic premise makes one wonder whether it would matter to him. That materialistic premise was implied just prior to the above excerpt. King wrote, "There certainly are physiological correlates [to the TM ritual], and we may be confident that in time science will discover them," as if, when science has discovered them, the moral issue the doctor's question raised would no longer exist. No doubt there are physiological correlates to the ritual of TM, but the Christian revelation affirms that there are also spiritual correlates to such rituals. Since the offerings in question are presented to the image of a man (Guru Dev) held to represent divinity, the spiritual correlates are those associated with idolatry—the spiritual oppression that results from violation of the Second Commandment (Exod. 20:4-6).

Aside from the few doing research that calls TM claims into question, scientists thus fall into two basic groups—the small group of those devoted to Maharishi and TM and a larger group who tend to accept TM as a useful relaxation technique though they may be more or less critical of Maharishi. Most scientists who are aware of TM have not concerned themselves greatly with the ethical issue of whether TM is being presented honestly when it is described as a nonreligious technique of relaxation.

It is reasonable to expect from science some clarity as to the physiological effects of TM if research continues at its present high rate for ten or twenty years. For long-term effects, studies covering the entire life span of meditating subjects will be necessary. We do not now have any such clarity on the basis of the small number of subjects tested; the short period of time of observation; and the absence of sufficient control data even to determine, in most cases, whether the effects measured are caused by TM or by other concurrent factors.

It is unreasonable to expect from science any clarity on the spiritual and moral effects of Eastern spiritual disciplines like TM. Science, after all, is generally understood to deal only with physical reality. That some scientists have insight at least into the ethical questions raised by the way TM is presented is to their credit. If scientists have not been particularly discerning of the spiritual and moral implications of TM, this is only evidence that the material dimension of life in which they specialize is not the only dimension. For insight into the spiritual dimensions of TM, then, we must look to another source. As a Christian, the writer has sought this insight from the written revelation of the actions and purposes of the God and Creator of the universe, the Bible. Further analysis of TM will be pursued explicitly in the light of the Biblical revelation.

Notes

1. Peter Fenwick, "100,000 Meditators Can't Be Wrong," *The Times Educational Supplement* (London), May 17, 1974 (MIU reprint).

2. Colin Campbell, Leon Otis, Gary Schwartz, "The Facts on Transcendental Meditation," *Psychology Today*, April 1974, pp. 37-46.

3. Ibid., p. 44.

4. Ibid., p. 46.

5. Leon Otis, "The Psychobiology of Meditation: Some Psychological Changes," as cited in *Everything You Want to Know About TM—Including How to Do It*, (New York: Pocket Books, 1976), John White, p. 56.

6. Jonathan Smith, unpublished doctoral dissertation, University of Michigan as cited in *Everything You Want to Know About TM—Including How to Do It*, White, p. 58.

7. Jonathan Smith, "Meditation as Psychotherapy: A Review of the Literature," *Psychological Bulletin*, vol. 82, no. 4, 1975, p. 562.

8. Ibid., p. 559.

9. David Rhinelander, "Disagreement at Institute Ends TM Use as Treatment," *The Hartford Courant* as cited in *Everything You Want to Know About TM—Including How to Do It*, White, pp. 63-64.

10. Maharishi, *On the Bhagavad-Gita*, A New Translation and Commentary (Baltimore: Penguin Books, 1967), p. 319.

11. Jack Forem, *Transcendental Meditation: Maharishi Mahesh Yogi and the Science of Creative Intelligence*, (New York: Dutton, 1973), p. 32.

12. Shankara, *Crest Jewel of Discrimination*, trans. Swami Prabhavananda and Christopher Isherwood (New York: New American Library, 1947), pp. 90 f.

13. Maharishi, *On the Bhagavad-Gita*, p. 98.

14. Forem, *Transcendental Meditation*, p. 104.

15. Ibid., p. 106.

16. Ibid., p. 101.

17. Herbert Benson and Robert K. Wallace, "Decreased Drug Abuse with Transcendental Meditation: A Study of 1862 Subjects," paper presented at the Drug Abuse International Symposium for Physicians, University of Michigan, Ann Arbor, Michigan, Nov. 10-13, 1970 (MIU reprint).

18. F. M. Brown, W. S. Stewart, and J. T. Blodgett, "EEG Kappa Rhythms During Transcendental Meditation and Possible Perceptual Threshold Changes Following," presented to the Kentucky Academy of Sciences, Richmond, Kentucky, Nov. 13, 1971, rev. Jan. 1972 (MIU reprint).

19. Schwartz, Psychology Today, April 1974, p. 40.

20. Otis, Psychology Today, April 1974, p. 45.

21. Smith, "Meditation as Psychotherapy," p. 559.

22. Herbert Benson, The Relaxation Response (New York: Morrow, 1975), p. 108.

23. Otis, Psychology Today, April 1974, p. 46.

24. Demetri P. Kanellakos and Jerome S. Lukas, The Psychobiology of Transcendental Meditation: A Literature Review (Menlo Park: Stanford Research Institute, 1973), p. 45.

25. Otis, Psychology Today, April 1974, p. 46.

26. Schwartz, Psychology Today, April 1974, p. 43.

27. Colin Martindale, "Creative People: What Makes Them So Different," Psychology Today, July 1975, p. 50.

28. Anonymous, "The TM Craze: Forty Minutes to Bliss," Time, Oct. 13, 1975, p. 74.

29. Benson, Relaxation Response, pp. 101-102.

30. Ibid., p. 103.

31. Paul H. Levine, "Transcendental Meditation and Science of Creative Intelligence," Phi Delta Kappan, Dec. 1972, p. 234 (MIU reprint).

32. Constance Holden, "Maharishi International University: 'Science of Creative Intelligence,'" Science, Mar. 28, 1975, pp. 1179-1180.

33. Anonymous, Time, Oct. 13, 1975, p. 74.

34. Herbert Benson, "Questions and Answers: Transcendental Meditation—Science or Cult?" Journal of the American Medical Association, Feb. 18, 1974, p. 807.

35. Lester S. King, Ibid.

CHAPTER FOUR

Transcendental Meditation: Faith and Enlightenment

by David Haddon

QUESTION: Why do many meditators come to stand in awe of Maharishi?

ANSWER: The aspect of devotion to Maharishi is publicly minimized by WPEC and SIMS as a matter of policy. Many meditators do revere Maharishi, nevertheless, because they believe him to be "enlightened." Mystical enlightenment is considered to be the attainment of an experimental knowledge of ultimate reality and truth in the altered ("exalted") states of consciousness discussed in chapter 2 (pp. 52-57). This "enlightenment" is the true goal of TM. Maharishi writes:

> Here is an important point for the practice of transcendental meditation. . . . the goal is to transcend that field [of activity], to arrive at transcendental consciousness, gain cosmic consciousness and ultimately rise to the consummation of all action in the state of Unity in God-consciousness.[1]

Many meditators, of course, begin TM with no devotion to Maharishi and little knowledge of or interest in enlightenment. They may continue TM merely for the incidental benefits of relaxation. They are, nevertheless, embarked on a program of "enlightenment" leading in a fixed progression from Transcendental-consciousness to Cosmic-consciousness, to God-consciousness, and, finally, to Unity. According to Maharishi again, "When a man begins transcendental meditation, he fulfills the conditions necessary for enlightenment."[2]

As a meditator begins to fall under the influence of this process of mystical enlightenment, devotion to Maharishi begins to grow. British physician Anthony Campbell, a former Catholic, exemplifies the kind of subdued adulation in which Maharishi is held by sophisticated devotees of TM. In his introduction to *Seven States of Consciousness* Campbell writes:

> I have become more and more convinced that Maharishi's coming out into the world with his system of meditation is by far the most important event of our time.[3]

Campbell expresses the underlying reason for this adulation as his faith in Maharishi's "enlightenment":

> Now, I have to admit that my experience of meditation has led me to *believe that the state of enlightenment does exist,* and if this is so it must afford a standpoint from which ultimate truth can be discerned. Maharishi, then, is a man who has a true vision of reality . . .[4] (emphasis added).

Campbell's experience of the altered states of consciousness produced by TM has led him *to faith in the existence of an enlightened state* just as Maharishi and his Hindu tradition teach. Having thus stated his faith in Maharishi's teaching, he goes on to say that Maharishi "is a man who has a true vision of reality," thus expressing his personal faith in his teacher as an "enlightened" man. Underlying Campbell's faith in Maharishi as teacher is a tacit faith in himself and in his own "experience of meditation."

Maharishi emphasizes the importance of faith in gaining "enlightenment" in a way that fits the pattern of Campbell's experience closely. Maharishi explains that

> the Lord [Krishna] names faith as a prerequisite to knowledge.
>
> There are three fields of faith: faith in oneself, faith in the teacher and faith in God. *Faith in oneself* is necessary so that one does not begin to doubt *one's own experience. Faith in the teacher* enables one to accept *the fundamentals of the teaching....* Faith in God [impersonal Being] protects man's heart and mind and ensures that steady progress which is so important in the life of a seeker.... For ultimate fulfilment in God-consciousness the greatest faith is needed[5] (emphasis added).

In the prior citations, Campbell expressed his faith in his "own experience" and in "teacher" and "teaching" just as they are here set forth by Maharishi as a "prerequisite to knowledge" (i.e., "enlightenment"). Campbell acknowledges that he has not attained to a high level of "enlightenment," but he has come to the prerequisite faith in Maharishi and in his teaching concerning the state of "enlightenment" and the nature of "God" as impersonal Being.

Such faith, then, is the *sine qua non,* or "prerequisite" of "enlightenment." It is not, of course, a requirement to begin TM, because the practice of TM itself is the means to faith. Maharishi writes that the regular practice of meditation . . . helps the heart and mind to grow in faith and keeps a man . . . on the path to enlightenment. . . . *the practice of transcendental meditation* is such that it can be started from whatever level of faith a man may have, for it *brings faith to the faithless* . . . [6] (emphasis added).

In Christianity it is well understood that faith in Christ comes from hearing what the Bible, God's Word, has to say about Christ. In TM, the corresponding means to faith is the practice of TM itself. Faith is another aspect of TM that is publicly minimized; but the inner reality is, that just as Maharishi says, "for ultimate fulfilment in God-consciousness the greatest faith is needed."

Meditators who through the practice of TM come to believe they are on the path of "enlightenment" also come to believe that Maharishi, as one who has come to the culmination of that path, has a "true vision of reality." As relative novices in the practice of consciousness "raising," they feel awe and gratitude to Maharishi as one who has both attained to the perfection of divinity in the "enlightened" state, and who has also generously made the means to "enlightenment" available to them and to the whole world in TM. Their faith in Maharishi leads naturally to devotion to him.

QUESTION: How is TM supposed to bring the meditator to a state of enlightenment?

ANSWER: In SCI, it is held that in TM the mind is brought to experience the subtlest level of the thought of the mantra until it transcends thought in the "Source of all thought" or Being (Brahman). The identity of the mind in the Transcendental (meditative) state with Being or "pure awareness" is directly

104

experienced. This, of course, is just another way of stating the Hindu doctrine of the identity of the self of man with the Self of the universe, which is expressed in a famous phrase from the Upanishads, "I am Brahman."

In Cosmic-consciousness, the identity of the self with the impersonal "God" is experienced not only while meditating, but also during waking and sleeping. In the still "higher" states, this sense of unity is directed outward toward the objects of perception so that finally a state is attained in which the unity of the self with all things is experienced. In the state of Unity, the statement that "All is One" is directly perceived as the deepest truth about reality. This mystical sense of unity is taken as the standard of truth about reality.

One effect of TM, then, is to alter permanently the meditator's view of the world until it harmonizes with and, indeed, seems to verify the monist world view of the unity of all things. Maharishi himself admits that TM is a conditioning process for this purpose. Concerning the "enlightened" state of Cosmic-consciousness, for example, he writes:

> This [state] is brought about by regularly interrupting the constant activity of the waking state of consciousness with periods of silence in transcendental consciousness [via TM]. When, through this practice, *the nervous system has been permanently conditioned* to maintain these two states together, then the consciousness remains always centered in the Self[7] (emphasis added).

According to Maharishi, then, TM is a conditioning process operating on the nervous system to transform one's perception of the world in a subjectively compelling way without the use of argument or evidence. It is particularly effective because the meditator—after the initiation itself—administers the conditioning process to himself.

Maharishi's claim that TM can permanently condition the nervous system so as to transform the very way reality is seen is a far cry from SIMS claim that TM is an innocent technique of relaxation. It has already been noted that Maharishi's rationalization for this deceptive procedure is the claim that the "ignorant" or unenlightened cannot understand the truth about reality (see pp. 8-9). The basis of this spiritual elitism in the Vedas is pointed out by physicist Paul Levine of the MIU faculty as follows:

> One of the most ancient expressions of man's wisdom, the Vedas (to which SCI traces its ancestry) hold that "knowledge is structured in consciousness," the implication being that the higher the level of consciousness the more profound the level of knowledge which can be owned.[8]

This concept of knowledge makes an absolute distinction between the "enlightened" and the "ignorant" on the basis of the consciousness alteration gained through meditation.

Maharishi's knowledge is thus so exclusive that those who have not been initiated in TM are not even considered able to comprehend it. Maharishi contends that this knowledge is essential for "the Lord [Krishna] declares that *realization of the state of all knowledge is the only way to salvation* and success in life; there is no other way"[9] (emphasis added). "Enlightenment," in fact, is declared to be the "only way to salvation." The myth that TM is compatible with all religions is thus exposed; TM is the key element in an exclusive system of "enlightenment."

The alternating of TM with normal activity, then, conditions the nervous system to the first stage of "enlightenment," or Cosmic-consciousness. The means to the still "higher" states of consciousness, however, include devotion to "God." Maharishi states that

> Cosmic-consciousness in turn develops into God-consciousness through devotion, the most highly refined type of action. . . . This is the blessing of action, that it leads one from the waking state of consciousness to transcendental pure consciousness, thence to cosmic-consciousness and finally to God-consciousness, the highest state of human evolution.[10]

> The teaching is that, having gained cosmic-consciousness . . . a man should devote himself to God and let the heart flow and overflow in love for Him, the great Lord of all.[11]

A person is not considered capable of true devotion to God until he has attained Cosmic-consciousness. For those who are entering this state, however, there is great personal distress. It may well be viewed as a self-induced state of schizophrenia. Maharishi admits that as

> . . . one begins to feel one's Self as separate from activity. This experience brings with it a feeling of confusion. . . . Doubts begin to arise in the mind. . . . Without proper understanding, even the direct experience of eternal freedom may be found to create confusion and fear.[12]

Why should the "direct experience of eternal freedom . . . create confusion and fear?" Faith in Maharishi's "enlightenment" is subject to reconsideration at this point as perhaps nowhere else. The meditator who persists commits himself to Maharishi by entering a supposedly irreversible state of consciousness.

Greg Randolph, a former TM teacher, describes the experience of a fellow meditator on entering Cosmic-consciousness as being

> unreal . . . like sitting in a drive-in movie. The movie is playing and you see the movie, but you really can't relate to the movie. This is what Cosmic-consciousness is—where you're actually sitting in this vastness, this world around you . . . and [are] not able to relate to it. . . . So this situation had an effect upon me making me ask, "Do I really want to reach this Cosmic-consciousness . . . [with this] alienation of yourself from the entire world around you? . . . The world around you becomes illusionary, becomes non-real. . . . This was one area that really convicted me.

Greg has become a Christian since his concern about the truth of Cosmic-consciousness led him to question his former trust in "Maharishi's being an enlightened person . . . having the key to wisdom and knowledge. . . ."

Since Maharishi admits that "enlightenment" is the result of a psycho-physiological conditioning process of the nervous system, a question that naturally arises is this: "Why should I trust my nervous system to hold the key to reality now that it has been subjected to a process of conditioning?" There is no guarantee that this particular conditioning process is leading to the truth. The fact that certain predicted and even beneficial results occur only shows that Maharishi and other yogis have traveled this path before us.

In reality, of course, it is not finally the nervous system of even the cosmically conscious meditator that is being trusted, but that of the fully "realized" man— in TM, Maharishi. Only the fully "enlightened" man is supposed to be in a position to judge these matters—yet his consciousness is the most highly conditioned of all. If the whole enterprise of consciousness "raising" is misguided, the "enlightened" man will be the last to notice it. The second question that arises is like the first: "Why should I trust my teacher's nervous system to hold the key to reality merely because it has been subjected to a rigorous process of conditioning?"

The seeker who subjects himself to the conditioning process leading to "enlightenment" must accept *on faith* both the teaching that "enlightenment" is the way to truth about reality and the claim that his teacher is "enlightened." The student, being unenlightened, is in no position to verify either claim. As Maharishi puts it, "The truth about a more advanced state of consciousness cannot be rightly evaluated from a lower level."[13] Thus, neither the value of "enlightenment" itself nor the "enlightened" state of any teacher can be determined by anyone in the system of "enlightenment" beneath the "enlightened" one. Evaluation of the system of "enlightenment" must of necessity come from a standpoint outside of the system. Such a standpoint is provided for Christians in the written record of the acts and commandments of the personal God and Creator, the Bible.

From the Biblical perspective, with its strong emphasis on truth telling, Maharishi's lack of candor about the religious aspects of TM raises an immediate question about the nature of his reputed "enlightenment." Maharishi publicly denies that TM has anything to do with religion, yet initiation into TM requires attendance at a religious ritual of worship to the gods of the Hindu Pantheon, and the writings of Maharishi explaining TM are filled with the doctrines of his Hindu tradition. Thus it is apparent that his state of "enlightenment" (which is supposed to produce only "spontaneous right action") does not lead him to tell the simple truth about his teaching. But if the "enlightenend" man does not spontaneously fulfill the most basic principle of human discourse and the Biblical standard ("Do not lie to each other" [Col. 3:9]) of truth telling, his supposed "raising" of consciousness has resulted in his own case in an obvious lowering of consciousness. Telling lies to promote the "truth" is a flight from truth and from reality in the area of morality.

TM, then, is said to bring a person to "enlightenment" through a systematic conditioning of the nervous system that finally causes the meditator to perceive reality in accord with the monist principle that "All is One." For the "higher" states beyond Cosmic-consciousness, devotion to "God" is a part of the conditioning process. The existence of the state of "enlightenment" cannot be verified by anyone not "enlightened" according to Maharishi's Vedic tradition because "knowledge is structured in consciousness." Great faith must be placed in the "enlightened" teacher who heads the system, because only he has the "true vision of reality." Since Maharishi doesn't practice truth telling with regard to TM, however, his consciousness obviously "falls short of the glory of God" as does that of all men according to the Bible (Rom. 3:23). Therefore Maharishi's and all other systems of "enlightenment" seeking "God-consciousness" through human effort are anti-Biblical.

QUESTION: If transcendental consciousness in TM and the states of "enlightenment" do not

**give an experience of ultimate reality,
what actually happens in them?**

ANSWER: "Transcendental consciousness" (the state
of awareness without thought or external perception,
attained from time to time while reciting the mantra in TM) can be understood in the light of psycho-
physiological research into the effects of uniform
stimulation on the nervous system. It seems that
uniform stimulation of one of the senses is equiva-
lent to *no stimulation* of the central nervous system
and has the effect of shutting down the stimulated
sense completely. If, for example, uniform visual stimulation is provided by taping white hemispheres
(halves of Ping-Pong balls were used in one experiment) over both eyes, the visual image quickly dis-
appears and the state of generally reduced awareness
of the external world and increased alpha brain wave
production characteristic of meditation occurs.[14]

The relation of the above experiment to the techniques of meditation in general is apparent. The repe-
titious stimulus of mantramic meditation (the mantra) approximates the uniform stimulus of the experiment with similar effects. Consciousness of the
outside world contacts, and conceptual thought become sporadic while an apparent inward expansion
may occur.

The alteration of consciousness resulting from this
suppression of both perception and thought by means
of repetition of the mantra eventually brings a striking experience of unity in which the self seems to
merge inwardly with the universe or ultimate reality.
This is the experience upon which the Hindu doctrine of the unity of the self of man and the Self of
the Universe is based. On the basis of this experience,

then, meditators are told that in TM they have direct experience of ultimate reality. This claim that the human nervous system can provide direct experience of "Reality" depends entirely on the unproven and inherently unprovable premise that man has immediate and unmediated access to ultimate reality or divinity within himself. However convincing the mystical experience may be subjectively, it can never prove this premise about man. The Biblical view of man as separated from God by the fall into sin which makes the mediation of Christ necesary for contact with the personal Father who is the transcendent, personal Reality, flatly rejects the monist premise of Hinduism that man by nature has direct access to God.

The Jewish philosopher and sometime mystic Martin Buber in *Between Man and Man* provides a cogent alternative interpretation for this kind of mystical experience:

> Now from my own unforgettable experience I know well that there is a state in which the bonds of the personal nature of life seem to have fallen away from us and we experience an undivided unity. But I do not know—what the soul willingly imagines and indeed is bound to imagine (mine too once did it)— that in this I had attained to a union with the primal being or the godhead. . . . I can elicit from those experiences only that in them I reached an undifferentiable unity of myself without form or content. . . . In the honest and sober account of the responsible understanding the unity is nothing but the unity of this soul of mine, whose "ground" I have reached . . . and not "the world of the All"; a defined and particular being and not "Being.". . .[15]

The basic experience of TM, therefore, is not an experience of infinite Being, but of the depersonalized unity of the meditator's own finite being. Actually, the meditator is merely experiencing his own altered consciousness which has been temporarily depersonalized by suppressing perceptions, intellect, and memory in meditation.

In the case of the "higher" states of consciousness, the inward experience of unity of Transcendental Consciousness is gradually turned outward until eventually the multiplicity of things in the world come to be experienced in a mystical unity with the meditator himself. This is the experience upon which the monist principle of the unity of Being ("All is One") is based. When the meditator sees himself in all things and all things in himself in accord with the Upanishadic maxim, "I am That, Thou art That, all This is nothing but That" ("That" is Brahman, the impersonal "God" of Hinduism), he has attained to Unity. Reason, then, is abandoned in favor of this mystical paradox, not as a matter of abstract principle, but because the cumulative effect of the conditioning process of TM on perception has brought the mind to a point where reality is experienced as unity. At this point the interference of meditation with logical thought is total in that reason is rejected in favor of mystical experience as the means for discerning truth about reality.

Except for the powerful subjective conviction aroused by mystical experience, there is no reason to accept the contradictory view of reality required by Hindu monism. To insist that the only reality is the transcendent One or, Brahman, leads to the contradictory affirmation that Brahman simultaneously is and is not the world. To be sure, the common, modern perception of the world as matter only is false. Meditators rightly reject such a constricted view of the universe. But there is no more reason to accept the Eastern monism of "spirit" than there is to accept the Western monism of matter. The third alternative of the Creator/creature duality revealed in the Bible is to be recommended to those whose experience of meditation has opened their minds to consider the realm of spirit. The meditator's experience that leads him to claim that the only reality is the unity of the Transcendent calls into question the materialist view that the only reality is the diversity of the material universe. Thus the meditator may come to be more open to consider the truth of Biblical revelation than is the materialist.

In TM, then, recitation of the mantra produces effects on the nervous system similar to experimental uniform stimulation of a sense. The practice of TM leads to a unitive mystical experience interpreted as the meditator's contacting Being (the "field of Creative Intelligence"). Martin Buber sees this experience merely as that of the unity of the meditator's own being or soul. Since the initial impression of unity with Being via TM is deceptive, the use of TM as a conditioning process (as Maharishi puts it) only extends the deception from inner experience to outer experience as well.*

QUESTION: What are the spiritual effects of the mystical enlightenment of TM?

ANSWER:

1. EFFECT ON CONSCIENCE

Many meditators and ex-meditators testify that TM relaxes the body and calms the mind. There is also some physiological evidence that TM lowers metabo-

---

*Portions of this answer were reprinted by permission from *His*, student magazine of Inter-Varsity Christian Fellowship, © 1973.

lism and calms the mind during its practice. For some people, at least, it seems that TM reduces tension and stress. For those who assume, as Maharishi does, that man's nature is basically good and who therefore blame tension and stress as the underlying causes of wrongdoing, TM may seem to be a solution to all human problems. This view is plausible also because tension and stress are known to produce physical pain and disease.

The Biblical revelation, however, points out that tension and stress in body and mind are often symptoms of wrongdoing rather than its cause. The psalmist describes the physical and mental symptoms of guilt for sin this way:

> My strength has failed because of my iniquity, And my body has wasted away (Ps. 31:10).

> There is no soundness in my flesh because of Thine indignation; There is no health in my bones because of my sin. For my iniquities are gone over my head; As a heavy burden they weigh too much for me. My wounds grow foul and fester. Because of my folly, I am bent over and greatly bowed down; I go mourning all day long. For my loins are filled with burning; And there is no soundness in my flesh. I am benumbed and badly crushed; I groan because of the agitation of my heart. Lord, all my desire is before Thee; And my sighing is not hidden from Thee. My heart throbs, my strength fails me; And the light of my eyes, even that has gone from me. . . . For I am ready to fall, And my sorrow is continually before me. For I confess my iniquity; I am full of anxiety because of my sin (Ps. 38:3-10, 17-18).

> When I kept silent about my sin, my body wasted away through my groaning all day long. For day and night Thy hand was heavy upon me; My vitality was drained away as with the fever-heat of summer. I ac-

115

knowledged my sin to Thee, And my iniquity I did not hide; I said, "I will confess my transgressions to the Lord"; And Thou didst forgive the guilt of my sin (Ps. 32:3-5).

Physical weakness or fatigue, weight loss, infection, slumped posture, severe depression, burning sensations, extreme anxiety, palpitations of the heart, dullness of eye, and other physical and mental effects of sin are described in these passages. The correct response to such distress in the confession of repentance together with God's response of forgiveness are described in the concluding verses of the passage from Psalm 32. In Biblical terms, it is conscience that activates the distressing responses to wrong behavior or sin described by the psalmist. The God-given purpose of conscience, however, is not to prolong such suffering, but to bring the sinner to repentance before God and man so that he can receive forgiveness and relief from the physical and mental distress of guilt.

In the *Christian Counselor's Manual,* Jay Adams defines conscience as

the God-given ability to evaluate one's own actions (Romans 2:15); and respond emotionally to that evaluation. . . . Pleasant or unpleasant physiological responses (visceral and otherwise) are activated as the result. . . . When we sin and our consciences evaluate the act or attitude as such, they next proceed to activate unpleasant visceral and other bodily responses to warn us to cease and desist and repent. God expects us to repent, confess our sins, and become reconciled to Him. Our future behavior must be changed by the Spirit to conform to the Word of God. Conscience evaluates such an actual course of action as the proper one, and eases up on the unpleasant physical responses. Taking pills, using alcohol or other drugs in order to

2. EFFECT ON INTELLECT

As noted earlier (pp. 112-113), the conditioning process of TM leads to a rejection of logical thought in favor of the subjective experience of the yogi as the means to learning the truth about reality. The world view that emerges from this experience as interpreted by Maharishi's tradition claims that there is only one Reality: transcendent and impersonal Being of which the world is only a temporary manifestation. This non-rational view of the universe is anti-Biblical as well as anti-intellectual. The claim of the universal oneness of Being contradicts the Biblical teaching of the fundamental duality of Creator and creature.

From a Biblical perspective, the continual repetition of a word, without regard for its meaning, used in TM to condition the meditator to accept the premise of universal oneness is particularly insidious. The "word" (the *logos*) is so highly regarded in the Bible that both the written Word of God itself and the living Word, Jesus Christ, are designated by this Greek term. In Greek, *logos* refers both to the written or spoken word and to the rational faculty. To systematically eliminate thought from the mind and to definitively reject it as a means to discovering the truth (of God's word revelation, the Bible, for example) is to attack the *logos* as rational faculty. To do so by means of the "meaningless repetition" of a mantra is to attack the *logos* as meaningful word as well. The rational faculty of hearing with understanding comes under assault. Since "faith comes from hearing the message, and the message is heard through the word of Christ" (Rom. 10:17), any practice that tends to the rejection of the very faculty by which faith in Christ is received is a virtual assault on the divine

119

Word Himself. It is, therefore, not surprising that the spiritual effect of TM is a spiritual dullness, like that in those to whom Jesus said:

> You will hear but never understand, you will look but never see, these people have become dull at heart and hard of hearing and have shut their eyes so that their eyes will never see, their ears never hear, or their hearts understand, and they will never turn to Me and let Me heal them" (Matt. 13:14-15, Beck).

In conversations with TM teachers and other meditators, I have sometimes noticed a seeming inability to grasp the difference between the monist claim of universal oneness as the nature of Reality and the Christian claim of an ultimate distinction between the nature of Creator and creature. Their conditioning has become so complete, it seems, that they are no longer able to understand a different viewpoint. This intellectual loss of the distinction between Creator and creature has the most serious spiritual effects. Unless a person realizes that God stands above His creation as Judge, he will never recognize his alienation from the Creator and his need for the mediation of the God-man, Jesus Christ. Without the mediation of Christ, men become confirmed in their alienation from God forever. The meditator is convinced by his experience and by the teaching that goes along with it that, far from being alienated from God, he is divine in his inner nature. The spiritual effect of this idea is the idolatry of self-worship.

TM, then, results in a rejection of the intellect as a means for discovering definitive truth about reality as Christians claim to do in the written revelation of the Bible. The world view that emerges from the conditioning process of meditation affirms a universal oneness implying human divinity. The spiritual effect of this view is to make the Christian revelation of the duality of Creator and creature incomprehensible to the meditator and to confirm him in his tendency as a fallen being to the idolatry of self-worship.

3. EFFECT ON WORLD VIEW

Through the ages the yogis of the Hindu tradition have developed various techniques of meditation to impose the unitary view of the universe on the mind despite its natural recalcitrance to it because of the contradictory evidence of ordinary experience. A primary purpose of meditation is to alter the meditator's perception and concept of reality to make them fit the unitary world view of Hindu cosmology. By undertaking a twice-daily routine of bringing the mind to a subjective experience of unity, the meditator subjects himself to a conditioning process with an inner dynamic well known to the yogis. Its tendency is to powerfully convince the meditator that: 1. in meditation he touches the deepest level of reality; 2. he experiences his own inner connection with divinity (Maharishi's unity of the individual self, *jiva*, with the cosmic Self, *Atman/Brahman*); 3. reality is unitary ("All is One."). Even if a secularized technique, such as that of Dr. Benson, is adopted for practical benefits only, these spiritually significant effects on the meditator's world view may be expected.

Dr. Benson's daring attempt to abstract a meditative technique from its religious framework must therefore be seen as spiritually hazardous. Since he largely ignores the ultimate meaning of the often striking meditative experience, there is a conceptual vacuum that, together with the inner dynamics of meditation, will tend to draw the meditator into one of the many mystical philosophies of human autonomy-divinity providing a plausible interpretation for the experience.

An interesting example is that of Flora Davis, who wrote an article in *Woman's Day* (August 1975) entitled, "I Taught Myself to Meditate." She taught herself to meditate using Dr. Benson's free-lance technique and later started TM to compare them. Although initially put off by the ritual and by the very mantra she was assigned, she came to prefer TM to the Benson technique because "it was just easier to stay with my secret mantra." In fact, she says, "By the last day of the lectures I was, to my own surprise, pretty much of a TM convert."[20] Her final conclusions are that

> after experimenting with several different techniques, I find I'm now hooked on meditation in general. I'm not sure why. . . . Perhaps I'm . . . intrigued by the prospect of someday achieving satori. . . . I am sure of only one thing: that meditation is a great pleasure for me. . . . Somehow it is . . . like "coming home"— home to myself.[21]

Flora Davis found her preference for TM over the free-lance technique surprising and her discovery that she is now "hooked on meditation" inexplicable. The latter discovery, however, is related to the idea that in meditation she comes home to herself. The concept of coming home to the self corresponds very well with the teaching of Maharishi's Brahmanism that the individual self comes to experience its true identity with the cosmic Self ("coming home . . . to myself") in meditation. For Flora Davis, then, Benson's technique was only a stepping stone to becoming a "TM convert" who finds "the prospect of someday achieving satori" intriguing. Given the spiritual dynamic of the practice of meditation, such results can be expected from Benson's Relaxation Response technique.

The effect of TM, and the techniques of yogic meditation in general, is to incline the meditator toward acceptance of a unitary view of the world, of the idea of human spiritual autonomy or divinity, and of meditation as the means to a knowledge of reality. The Christian world view rejects these ideas. It presents the world in terms of an ultimate distinction between the creation and its Creator. Man is therefore acknowledged to be a creature in need of a right relationship with his personal Creator. The means to this relationship is faith in the death of Christ for the sins of men. The practice of meditation and Christian faith are completely incompatible because of meditation's anti-Christian effect on the meditator's world view.

4. EFFECT ON SPIRITUAL EXPERIENCE

Another definite effect of TM is the opening of the meditator to the influence of spirits. In *Science of Being and Art of Living*, Maharishi warns against invoking spirits or acting as a medium because "to receive this ... power ... one must give oneself completely to that spirit's influence."[22] One reason that such a warning is necessary is that the meditative state resembles the passive state sought by mediums to facilitate contact with spirits. Another reason that demonic spirits may approach the meditator is that in the initiation ceremony he has involved himself in an idolatrous ritual. The apostle Paul explains the spiritual effect of idolatry:

> Do I mean then that ... an idol is anything? No, but the sacrifices of pagans are offered to demons, not to God, and I do not want you to be participants with demons (I Cor. 10:19-20).

In our discussion of the mantra in chapter 2 (p. 42), it was noted that although the mantras may be presented as meaningless sounds, Maharishi and another authority regard them as invocations of deity. In the light of the passage from I Corinthians, the deity invoked in such a pagan practice is demonic.

On the Christian view, then, the spirits Maharishi cautions against are demons and the hazard he warns about is demon possession. Meditators such as my co-author Vail testify to frightening encounters with spirits. On the general subject of the relation of yogic meditation to demon possession, Kent Philpott comments in his *Manual of Demonology and the Occult:*

> It has been a rather common experience in recent years to find middle class people becoming demon-possessed through such seemingly harmless practices as yoga meditation for weight-reducing and mind-relaxing, mind growth or awareness exercises, tapping into "alpha wave levels," and mental exercises aimed at achieving positive or creative thinking that center around a passive, calm, clear, or God-conscious state of mind.[23]

Real safety from evil spirits is to be found only through Jesus Christ, of whom the Scriptures reveal that, "the reason the Son of God appeared was to destroy the devil's work" (I John 3:8b).

QUESTION: What are the implications of Maharishi's proclamation of the Dawn of the Age of Enlightenment?

ANSWER: In January 1975, Maharishi announced the "Dawn of the Age of Enlightenment" at Lake Lucerne, Switzerland. He embarked on a five-continent tour to inform the world of the new age that he claims is beginning as a result of the spread of TM and SCI. The tour included appearances in five American cities in March 1975. Maharishi singled out San Francisco as the "First City of the Dawn of the Age of Enlightenment" during his appearance there because it has the highest proportion of meditators in its populace.

Drawing on an analogy from physics, as Maharishi often does, he claimed that just as the existence of a certain order among a few atoms of a substance will cause other atoms spontaneously to take on a similar order under certain conditions, so the practice of TM by a relatively small number of people will cause others who do not meditate to lead more orderly lives. The critical proportion is supposed to be 1 percent, or "one in one hundred." The latter phrase has become a slogan to express this concept. When the critical 1 percent of meditators has been reached in a given city, the crime rate, for example, is supposed to drop sharply. An average drop of 19 percent was claimed in one SIMS publication. Maharishi's followers call this claimed result the "Maharishi effect." Maharishi has long claimed that if 10 percent of the world's population practiced TM, the result would be world peace for generations. Now Maharishi is saying that positive effects from the practice of TM become socially and statistically discernible at a level of only 1 percent.

Nowhere has the role of faith in TM been more readily apparent than in Maharishi's presentation of purported sociological research in 360 cities in which TM is practiced by 1 percent or more of the population. He claimed that drug abuse, accidents, and illness, as well as crime, were all reduced in the 360 cities *because* 1 percent or more of the population of those cities were practicing TM. Only because of faith in Maharishi's teaching about the good effect of TM on society was such a correlation even thought of. And if the sought-for correlation was statistically obtained, it was still faith that pronounced the correlation to be a cause-and-effect relationship when there are a host of other uncontrolled variables of unknown effect.

The "Age of Enlightenment" has other, more ominous implications that go far beyond such dubious statistical correlations. As was pointed out in chapter 1 (p. 21), Maharishi seeks to use governments as a means to spread TM. An insight into his view of government is provided in the MIU publication *Address to Governments*. The introduction states:

> Every government is nearly all-powerful in its authority and has the resources of the entire country at its disposal and commands the services of all the most intelligent members of society.[24]

The view of government underlying this statement is contrary to the concept of constitutionally limited government of the Anglo-American tradition. It suggests a readiness to use government for any purpose whatever. Maharishi's view of the relation of government and religion in particular requires further consideration. On this subject, Maharishi has written:

> Religion in many countries seems to be either discredited or ignored by the governments whose constitutions have a secular basis. ... It is not enough to allow people to profess and practice their religion freely. *It is necessary that the authorities should be alert to see that the religion followed by the people produces in them the right spirit* of life and living. ... If religion fails to produce the effect it promises, then it needs help, and the national authority should ... provide that help.
>
> Transcendental meditation is the practice which en-

ables a man to live all that religions have taught through the ages; by this practice he easily rises to the level of divine Being and this brings fulfilment to all religions[25] (emphasis added).

Maharishi desires to see the "nearly all-powerful ... authority" of government used to "see that the religion followed by the people produces ... the right spirit." TM is the practice that will produce this "right spirit," says Maharishi.

The *Address* ... cited above continues: "It is the governments of the world who will implement the World Plan, and it is their action which will achieve its success." Seven steps recommended to the governments of the world to do this are: to establish MIU in their countries; to train teachers of SCI; to "introduce the teaching of Science of Creative Intelligence on all levels of the educational system"; to provide SCI and TM to all citizens, especially the military, police, medical personnel, and prison officials; to offer SCI to the Civil Service; to include SCI in the national health service; and to provide teaching of SCI to the public vía color TV.[26]

The agencies that MIU particularly wants to expose to TM are those that any group seeking political power wants to control: the schools, the military, the police, prison officials, medical personnel, and the civil service. When it is understood that a certain percentage of those exposed to TM continue it to the point of a relative "enlightenment" that convinces them that Maharishi is a fully "enlightened" one worthy of their devotion, love, and loyalty, the political implications of TM become apparent. Exposing a large number of people to TM results in the gradual emergence of a small core group of dedicated meditators whose primary loyalty is to Maharishi and his World Plan rather than to national governments or to their own traditional religious faith. When these meditators are drawn from influential positions in national life, they extend Maharishi's personal influence more widely.

What, then, is the character of the influence of Maharishi on government to be? It has already been seen that Maharishi is willing in principle to use government to "correct" religious teaching. A concrete example of Maharishi's approach to jurisprudence emerged on the April 1975 Merv Griffin Show interview. It was observed that a drug offender had been sentenced to four years of TM by a judge in Detroit, Michigan. Maharishi's enthusiastic and revealing comment was:

> This is the judgment of the Dawn of the Age of Enlightenment where the man is forced to develop his pure consciousness by law. This is the law of the Age of Enlightenment. By penalty he is forced to evolve.

If this is the judgment of the "Dawn" of the new age, what will be its judgment at high noon? Maharishi has said in the past that the one unchanging law should be "gain the knowledge of Science of Creative Intelligence and practice Transcendental Meditation ... ,"[27] but he has not directly stated what will become of those who reject the knowledge of SCI and the practice of TM as a matter of conscience.

Imposition of TM on an individual by judicial fiat, then, has already become a reality in a court in Michigan. That compulsory practice of TM is an appealing solution to judicial and social problems elsewhere is apparent from a letter written by Municipal Court Judge John E. Olsen of Ashtabula, Ohio, and publicized by SIMS. Judge Olsen writes to the Prison Board

of Erie, Pennsylvania, that "personally I am very de-
sirous of initiating a required submission to 'TM'
among drug abusers, but have not yet reached a satis-
factory method to accomplish a mandatory submission."

Before he developed his own meditation technique,
meditation researcher and physician Herbert Benson
also advocated mandatory attendance at TM instruction for an experimental group of drug addicts. In an
enclosure to a 1971 letter to the Chairman of the
House Select Committee on Crime concerned with
narcotics research, rehabilitation, and treatment, Benson recommended that an experimental group of narcotics addicts be subjected to instruction in TM on
a required basis to determine "the effect of required
transcendental meditation on such usage of [nar-
cotics]. . . ."[28]

In this country, then, Maharishi has not been alone
in advocating compulsion in the spread of TM. In
Canada, however, one school has even adopted SCI
as a compulsory course. The *Ecole Polyvalente Marcel-
Landry* in Montreal was the first school to make SCI
a mandatory subject. It is to be hoped, as the religious
nature of TM becomes clear, that the First Amend-
ment guarantees of religious liberty will provide an
insurmountable obstacle to compulsory TM in U.S.
courts and schools.

From the willingness of Maharishi and others to
make TM compulsory, it appears that there is in TM's
promise of an "Age of Enlightenment" a potential for
a spiritually based authoritarianism that would require
the universal practice of TM in accordance with Maharishi's one unchanging law cited above. That the
proponents of TM speak of laws imposing TM now
while the "Age of Enlightenment" is just dawning

provides a clue as to what their attitude may be should they gain a greater measure of influence. Of those who prove uncooperative in receiving "enlightenment" Maharishi has written:

> There has not been and there will not be a place for the unfit. The fit will lead, and if the unfit are not coming along there is no place for them. In the place where light dominates there is no place for darkness. In the Age of Enlightenment there is no place for ignorant people.[29]

That this statement represents the considered judgment of Maharishi is borne out by its consistency with his interpretation of the *Bhagavad-Gita* (4, 18) to say that " 'men' are those who have realized ... the truth" and that "one who has not realized the truth ... does not deserve to be called a man."[30] The "truth," of course, is realized by means of TM, according to Maharishi. The "fit" who practice TM are here distinguished from the "unfit" who reject TM as the human from the subhuman. The practice of TM thus becomes grounds for a new discrimination between those considered to be truly human who will lead (i.e., rule) and the rest who are considered to be subhuman.

What would become of those who object to the knowledge of SCI and the practice of TM on the grounds of conscience under the regime of the "Age of Enlightenment"? That would be spontaneously determined by the fully "enlightened" man whose consciousness is supposed to have evolved until it offers "an absolute basis for right action."[31] He is attuned to the upward evolution of consciousness so as to automatically choose action in accord with the (relativistic) criterion: "All that is good which helps the

130

process of evolution. . . . Bad [is] . . . opposite to the path of evolution."[32] Any refusal to practice TM is opposed to the path of consciousness evolution—hence is evil. Therefore those who oppose SCI and TM are evil and could be dealt with just as the warrior Arjuna was counseled to deal with his evil opponents in the *Bhagavad-Gita*. In his commentary on this poem, Maharishi approvingly describes the necessity of Arjuna's attaining

> a state of consciousness which will justify any action of his and will allow him even to kill in love, in support of the purpose of evolution.[33]

Maharishi's own description of what is to become of the "unfit" who may oppose SCI and TM cited in part above continues:

> The ignorant will be made enlightened by a few orderly, enlightened people moving around. Nature will not allow ignorance to prevail. It just can't. Non-existence of the unfit has been the law of nature.[34]

According to Maharishi, then, there is "no place for the ignorant," and "there will not be a place for the unfit." Their "non-existence . . . has been the law of nature."

One political implication of the system of "enlightenment" through raising consciousness to the level of divinity by meditation is the dedication of government to the end of spreading the doctrine of "enlightenment" throughout the world. Another implication of Maharishi's "Age of Enlightenment" is the elimination of those who oppose the evolution of consciousness by means of SCI and TM either by their compulsory "enlightenment" or by "killing in love." Maharishi has never advocated killing his opponents, of course, but it is perfectly consistent with his philosophy. There is nothing in Maharishi's doctrine to prohibit killing those who demonstrate their "evil" counter-evolutionary character by opposing the advance of TM. Any means may be used for the advancement of "enlightenment" because the state of "enlightenment" itself is the only absolute.

In the Hindu monism of Maharishi's tradition, the individual has no lasting significance since he is only a temporary manifestation of the Absolute. The god Krishna encourages Arjuna to "kill in love" because the Absolute (Being or Brahman) cannot be slain, whatever may happen to the body in which it temporarily dwells. Maharishi comments that

> the Lord [Krishna] begins by making him [Arjuna] understand that [his opponents'] . . . existence would not, in the real sense, be destroyed by his weapons. Reality . . . cannot be slain.[35]

If an "Age of Enlightenment" such as Maharishi envisions should ever come to pass, Christians who remain faithful to the Biblical revelation in preference to mystical "enlightenment" can expect ruthless persecution. Such an age would again fulfill Jesus' words to His disciples that "a time is coming when anyone who kills you will think he is offering a service to God" (John 16:2).

Notes

1. Maharishi, *On the Bhagavad-Gita: A New Translation and Commentary* (Baltimore: Penguin Books, 1967), p. 301.
2. Ibid., p. 317.
3. Anthony Campbell, *Seven States of Consciousness: A Vision of Possibilities Suggested by the Teaching of Maharishi Mahesh Yogi* (London: Gollancz, 1973), p. 30.
4. Ibid., p. 13.
5. Maharishi, *On the Bhagavad-Gita*, pp. 316-317.
6. Ibid., pp. 317, 319.
7. Ibid., p. 226.
8. Paul H. Levine, "Transcendental Meditation and Science of Creative Intelligence," *Phi Delta Kappan*, Dec. 1972, p. 234 (MIU reprint).
9. Maharishi, *On the Bhagavad-Gita*, pp. 228-229.
10. Ibid., p. 193.
11. Ibid., p. 162.
12. Ibid., p. 320.
13. Ibid., p. 449.
14. Claudio Naranjo and Robert E. Ornstein, *On the Psychology of Meditation* (New York: Viking Press, 1971), pp. 163-167.
15. Martin Buber, *Between Man and Man* (New York: Macmillan, 1965), p. 24.
16. Jay Adams, *The Christian Counselor's Manual* (Nutley, New Jersey: Presbyterian and Reformed Publishing Co., 1973), pp. 94-95.
17. Maharishi, *On the Bhagavad-Gita*, p. 299.
18. Ibid., p. 166.
19. Maharishi, *The Science of Being and Art of Living*, rev. ed. (Los Angeles: International SRM Publications, 1967), p. 173.
20. Flora Davis, "I Taught Myself to Meditate," *Woman's Day*, Aug. 1975, p. 76.
21. Ibid., p. 78.
22. Maharishi, *The Science of Being*, p. 106.
23. Kent Philpott, *A Manual of Demonology and the Occult*, (Grand Rapids: Zondervan, 1973), p. 44.
24. Anonymous, *An Address to Governments*, p. 8.
25. Maharishi, *The Science of Being*, p. 262.
26. Anonymous, *An Address to Governments*, p. 23.

27. Maharishi, "Maharishi Mahesh Yogi and the Science of Creative Intelligence: A Transcript of a National Television Interview," *The Western TM Reporter*, p. 12.
28. Herbert Benson, "Preliminary Research Proposal" in *The Congressional Record*, "Hearings before the Select Committee on Crime, House of Representatives, 92nd Congress, First Session, June 2, 3, 4, and 23, 1971." Serial No. 92-1. (Washington, D.C.: U.S. Government Printing Office, 1971) in an untitled booklet of scientific research reprints, (MIU, 1973), p. 7.
29. Pam Porter, "And the Fit Shall Lead," *Atlanta Gazette*, April 2, 1975, p. 17.
30. Maharishi, *On the Bhagavad-Gita*, p. 279.
31. Maharishi, *The Science of Being*, p. 173.
32. Maharishi, *Meditations of Maharishi Mahesh Yogi* (New York: Bantam Books, 1968), p. 33.
33. Maharishi, *On the Bhagavad-Gita*, p. 76.
34. Pam Porter, "And the Fit Shall Lead," p. 17.
35. Maharishi, *On the Bhagavad-Gita*, p. 101.

CHAPTER FIVE

Transcendental Meditation: Maharishi's Theology in Christian Perspective

by David Haddon

QUESTION: What does Maharishi teach about God?

ANSWER: In *Science of Being and Art of Living,* Maharishi writes that

> God is found in two phases of reality: as a supreme Being of absolute eternal nature and as a personal God at the highest level of phenomenal creation, the celestial level of creation. Thus God has two aspects: the personal and the impersonal. They are the two realities of the word God.[1]

Thus the impersonal aspect of God is the "supreme Being of absolute, eternal nature," while the personal aspect of God is relegated to the "level of phenomenal creation."

THE PERSONAL GOD

Maharishi's personal God, like the rest of creation of which it is a part, is only a temporal or relative

135

manifestation of the impersonal aspect of God. Therefore the personal God is not eternal. Maharishi writes that

> with the dissolution of creation the almighty, personal God also merges into the impersonal, absolute state of the Supreme. . . .[2]

Since Maharishi doesn't recognize the personal God as eternal and absolute in supremacy, his teaching about God is incompatible from the outset with the monotheistic faiths. Christianity, for example, affirms the existence of but one eternal, personal God, the Creator and Sustainer of the universe.

Since the impersonal aspect of God is considered supreme in Maharishi's Hindu tradition, "It" receives most of his attention. Maharishi's view of the personal God, on the other hand, suffers from great uncertainty. Maharishi reasons that

> God in personal form . . . can only be "He" or "She." . . . Some say It is both "He" and "She," but certainly It is not "It" because of the personal character ("It" refers to the impersonal "God").

Such confusion about the gender of the personal God shows that Maharishi lacks direct experience of and relationship with the personal God. Instead of an authoritative word about God, he offers speculation ("God . . . can only be 'He' or 'She.'") and the opinion of others ("Some say It is both 'He' and 'She'. . .").

For Maharishi, indeed, the personal God sometimes seems to be a kind of projection of human faculties onto a "big Man in the sky." He states, for example, that

> this one supreme, personal Being would have a nervous system so highly developed that His ability on

> every level of life would be unlimited. His senses
> would be the most powerful senses, His mind the most
> powerful mind, His intellect the most powerful in-
> tellect, His ego the most powerful ego.[4]

Maharishi's previously noted uncertainty about the
nature of the personal God emerges once again in his
discussion of the perfection of this God's "senses." He
is uncertain about whether the personal God has
sense organs or not for he speculates that

> when we say perfection of the senses we mean that if
> He has eyes, His eyes will be perfect in the sense that
> they will be able to see all things at one time. If He
> has a nose, His nose will be able to smell all the va-
> rieties of smells at one time. If He has ears, His ears
> will be able to hear all the sounds of the entire cosmos
> at one time.[5]

Maharishi lapses into such speculative absurdities because his tradition lacks a clear word of revelation
from the infinite-personal God about Himself. From
the Biblical revelation it is clearly understood that
the invisible, personal God is spirit and as such has
no need of sense organs to sustain His omniscience
(John 4:24).

On the other hand, Maharishi has some truth about
the nature of God, for he continues the above passage
as follows:

> His almighty mind will naturally be aware of anything
> on any level at any time. His almighty intellect will be
> able to decide everything at any moment. All the in-
> numerable decisions that are the apparent results of
> natural laws in the process of evolution are the in-
> numerable decisions of the almighty, personal, su-
> preme God at the head of creation. He governs and
> maintains the entire field of evolution and the separate
> lives of innumerable beings in the whole cosmos.[6]

This description of God's omniscience and providence is not so far from the Biblical revelation of Psalm 139. Aside from the premise that the personal God is a part ("the head") of creation, the main unorthodox element from a Christian viewpoint is the substitution of the "process of evolution" for God's foreknowledge and predestination as the means of His providence.

So even though Maharishi's tradition lacks Biblical revelation, it has considerable knowledge of the nature of the personal God, just as the apostle Paul affirms:

> What may be known about God is plain to them, because God has made it plain to them. For since the creation of the world God's invisible qualities—his eternal power and divine nature—have been clearly seen, being understood from what has been made, so that men are without excuse (Rom. 1:19-20, NIV).

Maharishi, indeed, affirms that "to refute the existence of the personal God can only be the result of an undeveloped state of mind."[7] Maharishi, then, is not ignorant of the existence of the personal God. In denying the *"eternal* power" of the personal God by relegating Him to the level of the temporal creation, however, he shares in the universal failure of men to give due honor to the personal Creator whose existence is "plain to them." This failure is revealed in the verses of Scripture immediately following those cited above:

> For although they knew God, they neither glorified him as God nor gave thanks to him, but their thinking became futile and their foolish hearts were darkened. Although they claimed to be wise, they became fools and exchanged the glory of the immortal God

for images made to look like mortal man and birds and animals and reptiles (Rom. 1:21-23, NIV).

In the initiation ceremony of TM, the "glory of the immortal God" is literally exchanged for a painted image of Maharishi's dead teacher, Guru Dev. Before the image of this "mortal man," the flowers, fruit, and white cloth brought by novice meditators are offered on an altar, and participants assume the kneeling posture of worship. These acts of worship are performed because Guru Dev is considered to be a personal manifestation of divinity in Maharishi's tradition.

Unfortunately, just as the apostle reveals, the elements of truth contained in Maharishi's teaching about God have not led him to acknowledge the personal God as supreme so as to avert the "wrath of God" which, the apostle warns, "is being revealed from heaven against all the godlessness and wickedness of men who suppress the truth by their wickedness" (Rom. 1:18, NIV). Instead, Maharishi joins in suppressing the truth about God by denying the eternal nature of the personal God (whom he says is subject to the dissolution of the creation) and by seeking to realize his own supposed identity with "God" by means (TM) that even require ritual acts of idolatry.

THE IMPERSONAL GOD

Maharishi, then, brings no word of revelation from the personal God whose importance to his system is minimal. Neither does he bring a word of revelation spoken by the Being he regards as supreme, because "It" is not a person capable of speech. Maharishi admits the impotence of this Being, the impersonal "God," as far as the activities of thinking, loving, and acting, of which even the humblest person is capable. He writes of "It" that

139

the Absolute is said to be almighty but . . . being everything, It cannot do anything or know anything. It is
beyond doing and knowing. It is almighty in the sense
that without It nothing would exist.[8]

Even though "It" is impotent to act or know, the
impersonal "God" is here set forth as the "almighty"
cause of all that exists ("without It nothing would
exist"). But if causality is attributed to anything, the
principles of causality may be invoked. One such
principle would indicate that a cause must be at least
as great as its supposed effect. To explain the existence of the universe and man in terms of causality,
then, what is required is not just a Being postulated
to be greater in extent and energy than the effect,
but a Being of infinite wisdom and power having
precisely those abilities of knowing and doing admit-
tedly absent from Maharishi's Absolute. The personal
being of man in particular requires a personal cause
to account for his ability to think, love, and act, and
to put these into a moral context. The quantum jump
upward from impersonal Being to such a personal
being as man cannot be accounted for by the monist
such as Maharishi any more than by the materialist.
Both are faced with the absence of a satisfying answer
to the question of ultimate origins.[9]

A genuine theist who acknowledges the personhood
of the Supreme Being has, by contrast, a *reasonable
explanation* for the existence of the universe and for
man in the personal God who is infinite in wisdom
and in power to act. If the theist is a Christian, he
also has *valid historical evidence* for the existence of
the personal God who is supreme: the life, death, and
resurrection of the Son of God, Jesus Christ, recorded
in those ancient documents, the Gospels. The Christian has, in addition, *his personal experience* of the

140

forgiveness of his sins and of his new relationship as a child of God the Father through the personal Spirit of God, the Holy Spirit.

The Christian answer to the question of ultimate origins in the person of the infinite God unites the two strands of truth of God's personhood and of God's infinitude which have been divided by Maharishi's tradition of monism. It is important to see that both of these elements of truth about God are present in his tradition. The truth of God's personhood is represented by Maharishi's personal "God," and the truth of God's infinitude is represented by Maharishi's impersonal "God." Distortion enters because, despite its emphasis on oneness, the monist tradition of Maharishi divides the personal from the infinite in God. Therefore Maharishi fails to acknowledge that the one eternal God is simultaneously personal and infinite.

The reason for the division of the personal from the infinite in Maharishi's tradition was touched upon above in the discussion of Maharishi's personal God. Since his Vedic tradition lacks a clear word of revelation concerning the personal God, Maharishi tends to imagine that the personal God is like man on a superior scale. Since man is personal and as such is finite and limited, Maharishi and his tradition conclude that the personal God must also suffer limitation. But there is no necessary contradiction between personality and infinitude including eternity of existence. Since all personal beings except the personal God are also finite and temporal, however, unless one has received the special revelation of the Bible concerning the infinite-personal God, he may easily assume that all personal beings are finite. The result in Maharishi's tradition, lacking as it does God's written revelation, has been the division of God into a personal aspect that is considered to be temporal and an impersonal aspect that is considered to be eternal and supreme. Ironically, it is in conjunction with the denial of the true duality between God and His creation by the Vedic tradition, that this false duality of personality and infinitude is introduced into the concept of God. When a meditator who is pursuing spiritual fulfillment in TM comes to understand the Biblical revelation that the Being he is seeking is personal as well as infinite and distinct from the creation, including man, the rationale of the practice of TM is undermined. If complete fulfillment is found in the transcendent, personal God, an impersonal technique of contacting an impersonal "God" supposedly residing within man is of no value in the pursuit of God.

The concept of the impersonal "God" of the monist tradition of Shankara does bear the truth of the infinitude of God, but it is largely the construction of imagination working with the materials of mystical experience. Maharishi, following this mystical tradition, teaches that ultimately there is only one thing in the universe, that "All is One," Being or Brahman. Because it is impersonal, it is referred to by the neuter pronoun "It." In the Science of Creative Intelligence, "It" is called the "field of Creative Intelligence."

The impersonal "God" is said to be incomprehensible to the mind and indescribable, since "It" has no limitations and thus lacks all attributes. "It" is described, nevertheless, in three Sanscrit words, "Sat-Chit-Ananda." These words are commonly rendered as "Being-Intelligence-Bliss," but Maharishi prefers to translate them as "eternal," "consciousness," "bliss."[10]

These descriptive words for the "indescribable" Being arise in a readily understandable way from the mystical experience induced by the meditation that underlies this tradition. The mystical experience of unity attained from time to time in TM induces *a loss of the sense of the passage of time* while a contentless and hence *depersonalized state of consciousness* is maintained along with occasional *sensations of bliss*. Thus the elements of the description of Being or the impersonal "God" as *eternal-consciousness-bliss* are simply descriptions of the subjective state of the meditator in TM. Because the meditator's conscious sense of time is suspended in TM, Being is considered to be *timeless* or "eternal." Since a *depersonalized consciousness* is retained in the meditative state, *depersonalized* or *impersonal* "consciousness" is attributed to Being. And since the meditator's experience of the meditative state commonly ranges from a pleasant euphoria to ecstatic bliss in those who pursue it diligently and successfully, Being is also described as "bliss" in its inner nature. The entire characterization of Being or "God" as impersonal *eternal-consciousness-bliss* is the result of absolutizing the meditator's subjective experience of meditation.

Why, then, has Maharishi's tradition absolutized the experience of meditation? It is characteristic of mystical experience in general that it induces a strong, subjective conviction that in it the ultimate reality has been experienced. The tradition of Maharishi has accepted the yogi's subjective impression at face value; it takes the conclusions about the nature of ultimate reality as impersonal Being characterized as *eternal-consciousness-bliss* to be proven by the "direct experience" of the meditative state. It is apparent from the above discussion that these conclusions can be explained as unwarranted extrapolations of the yogi's subjective impressions in the meditative state. These conclusions depend entirely on the assumption about man of that which is yet to be proved: that man in himself has access to the ultimate reality, or "God."

The feeling of certainty given by this mystical experience, nevertheless, can be overwhelming. As Maharishi puts it, "The experience of absolute Being leaves no doubt about the essential constituent of the whole structure of creation."[11] Convincing as the experience is to some meditators, it provides no evidence for the claim made for it. Because of its convincing nature, however, those who start TM for nonspiritual reasons, such as relaxation, are vulnerable to conversion to TM as a spiritual pursuit and as a way of life. Maharishi's object in offering TM as widely as possible is the making of as many such converts as possible. These converts are the ones who may become teachers of TM and work to fulfill Maharishi's World Plan.

Not only is there no objective evidence for the existence of this "absolute Being," "It's" very postulated existence involves logical contradiction. Maharishi exposes the contradictory nature of this Being (Brahman) in these words:

> Brahman, which is an all-pervading mass of bliss, does not exhibit any quality of bliss. . . . Brahman is that which cannot be expressed in words, even though the Upanishads use words to educate us about Its nature. In the field of speech, Brahman lies between two contrary statements. It is absolute and relative at the same time. It is the eternal imperishable even while It is ever-changing. It is said to be both this and That. It is spoken of as Sat-Chit-Ananda but includes what is not Sat, what is not Chit and what is not Ananda. . . . [It is] a "wonder," for it is not anything that can be

144

conceived of intellectually; it is not anything that can be appreciated by emotion.[12]

Thus Brahman simultaneously is and is not: bliss, absolute, imperishable, "Sat-Chit-Ananda." To accept this view of reality requires the abandonment of rational understanding with regard to ultimate truth, even though, of course, it must be retained for purposes of daily living. The fundamental contradiction involved springs from absolutizing the unitive mystical experience from which the basic premise of monism that "All is One" arises. It follows that the One—transcendent Being or Brahman—must simultaneously be the universe (since there is only one Thing) and not be the universe (since Being transcends the universe absolutely). This view is so contrary to normal perception, ordinary experience, and reason that few would accept it except that the practice of meditation over an extended period conditions the mind to perceive the world in accordance with it (see pp. 104-132).

Maharishi's tradition is caught in this morass of contradiction because of its failure to distinguish the Creator from the creation. We have seen earlier that Maharishi explicitly identifies the personal God with a part of the creation, the "celestial level of creation." The impersonal "God" or Being is inevitably identified with the entire creation. Maharishi thus writes that "all the different strata of creation are made of that substance which is called absolute Being."[13] Elsewhere he explains that "impersonal, absolute Being, or God, pervades all fields of existence as the essential constituent of creation."[14] So Maharishi considers that "God" is the "substance" or "essential constituent" of creation. Maharishi's identification of "God" and the "substance" of creation exposed above arises from taking the unitive state of consciousness induced by TM to be the ultimate criterion of truth.

Christianity, by contrast, takes the written Word of the personal God who is absolute and supreme in Himself as its ultimate criterion of truth. God's Word reveals that though He is omnipresent within His creation in His personal fullness, He is entirely distinct in substance from His creation. The universe was created *out of nothing* by the will and power of the personal Creator through His creative word. The Scriptures record that "by the word of the Lord were the heavens made; and all the host of them by the breath of his mouth. . . . For he spoke and it was done; he commanded and it stood fast" (Ps. 33:6, 9). The New Testament makes the same revelation: "By faith we understand that the universe was formed at God's command, so that what is seen was not made out of what was visible" (Heb. 11:3, NIV).

The personal God and Creator, then, is distinct from the creation He spoke into existence and absolutely transcends it in His supremacy over "the heavens and the earth." The psalmist sings,

> The Lord is high above all nations, and his glory above the heavens! Who is like the Lord our God, who is seated on high, who looks far down upon the heavens and the earth? (Ps. 113:4-5, RSV). For Thou, O Lord, art most high above all the earth; Thou transcendest far above all gods (Ps. 97:9, MLB). The Lord is majestic in Zion; He is supreme . . . (Ps. 99:2, MLB).

In the light of the Biblical revelation of the transcendence of God, Maharishi's confusion of Creator and creation at both the personal and impersonal levels of "God," dishonors the personal Creator revealed in the Bible by identifying Him with that which He has made. Such confusion is spiritually dangerous because it impels men toward those religious practices that fulfill the Biblical definition of idolatry: to worship and serve the creation rather than the Creator.

Quite aside from the idolatrous ritual of the initiation ceremony, TM leads the meditator toward the idolatry of self-worship as a result of the identification of the self of the meditator with the "Self" of the entire creation. The dynamic of the meditative state brought the yogis of Maharishi's tradition to this idolatrous identification of God and His creation long ago. TM gradually tends to the same result. Therefore Christians should oppose TM as they oppose any form of idolatry.

To sum up Maharishi's teaching about God, he says that God exists on a personal level as part of the creation and on an impersonal level which is supreme. The impersonal "God" (called variously Being, the Absolute, Brahman, and in SCI the "field of Creative Intelligence") is indescribable, yet is characterized as *eternal-consciousness-bliss*. Despite the logical contradiction, Being is said to be both eternal and temporal, transcendent of the universe and the "substance" of which it is made. Being, or the impersonal "God," is therefore to be found in everything and everyone.

The Biblical view of God, by contrast, presents the personal God as supreme and as absolutely independent of His creation of which He forms no part, though He is omnipresent throughout in His personal fullness and constantly sustains it by the word of His power (Heb. 1:3). The personal God is therefore not subject to the dissolution of the creation (as Maharishi teaches) because He exists eternally. Of the personal Creator the psalmist declares:

> Of old hast thou laid the foundation of the earth: and the heavens are the work of thy hands. They shall perish, but thou shalt endure; yea, all of them shall wax old like a garment; as a vesture shalt thou change them, and they shall be changed: But thou art the same, and thy years shall have no end (Ps. 102:25-27, AV).

> Before the mountains were brought forth or ever thou hadst formed the earth and the world, even from everlasting to everlasting, thou art God. (Ps. 90:2, AV).

The endless existence of the personal God from eternity to eternity is here plainly set forth.

The eternal, personal God revealed in the Bible as the only true God, the Creator and Sustainer of the universe, never acknowledges man as God or as a part of God. The exclusive personal claim to deity of the Lord, Jehovah, is proclaimed by the Hebrew prophets. Isaiah, for example, declares: "Thus says the Lord, who created the heavens (he is God!)....'I am the Lord, and there is no other'" (Isa. 45:18, RSV). Thus Isaiah flatly contradicts Maharishi's view of the supreme Being as the impersonal "constituent" of creation such that everything and everyone is a part of God. God always is a Person in His own right and is distinct from all other persons and beings He as "the Lord" has made. Because God is personal, He has communicated to man what man needs to know about God in words that have been written in a book. Rather than mystical experience, this book, the Bible, is the objective criterion of truth about God.

QUESTION: What does Maharishi teach about man's nature and purpose?

ANSWER: According to Maharishi, "Simplicity and innocence are already deeply rooted in the very nature of each individual."[15] He considers human nature, then, to be basically good. And just as he takes the unitive state as the absolute norm from which to describe the nature of "God," Maharishi takes the same state as the norm from which to describe the nature of man. Because the same state defines both "God" and man, it follows that man is not only "innocent" but also "divine." Man's basic problem or "sin" is his ignorance of the experience of his own divinity. Man's purpose is to experience his own divinity by means of TM.

The message of man's divinity is close to Maharishi's heart and essential to the real rationale for practicing TM. Maharishi explicitly affirms the identity of man and the impersonal "God" as follows:

> The impersonal God is the Being which dwells in the heart of everyone. *Each individual is, in his true nature, the impersonal God.* That is why the Vedic philosophy of the Upanishads declares: "I am That, thou art That, and all this is That."[16] (Emphasis added. "That" refers to "God" or Brahman.)

In another book he writes:

> The Divine Plan of today is to inform the people that it is simple . . . for everyone to begin to enjoy his own inner Divine Nature. . . . You are Divine. . . . For man there is no reason to suffer in life, because he is in himself Divine Consciousness. He himself is the Absolute Bliss, the great power, the great reservoir of all energy, peace and happiness. He is That[17] (emphasis added).

Once more, Maharishi writes that "man on earth, a man of a real, lively and integrated religion, should be a living god, the Divine speaking...."[18]

Just as many Western religious leaders influenced by Eastern concepts of God do, Maharishi attempts to use Biblical authority to support his claim for man's divinity. Seizing on a phrase from Psalm 46, Maharishi mistakenly attributes it to Christ, then quotes and interprets it as follows:

> "Be still and know that I am God." Be still and know that you are God and when you know that you are God you will begin to live Godhood....[19]

Maharishi and others apply this Scripture entirely outside of its context of Hebrew language and religion to the state of stillness of Eastern meditation in which the meditator is led to believe that he experiences his own divinity. In its context in Psalm 46, however, it is apparent that this Scripture is a call to acknowledge the divinity not of the self but of the personal and transcendent God of Biblical revelation, the Lord of hosts. The verse and its following context are:

> "Be still, and know that I am God. I am exalted among the nations, I am exalted in the earth!" The Lord of hosts is with us; the God of Jacob is our refuge (Ps. 46:10-11, RSV).

Biblical authority does not support the claim of man's divinity, and neither does common experience. If man were divine, as Maharishi claims, it would seem that there shouldn't be the hatred, violence, and conflict that are so prominent in human history. Maharishi has to acknowledge that man as he is has a problem. According to Maharishi, man has forgotten his inner divinity through the loss of the simple technique of experiencing it. The lost technique is TM. He writes that

> meditation makes that connection ["with the source"] on the conscious level. . . . Otherwise, although we are all 100% Divine, consciously we do not know that we are Divine; so then there is no connection, there is no bridge and we suffer on the conscious level.[20]

Elsewhere Maharishi contends that

> all suffering is due to ignorance of a way to unfold the divine glory which is present within oneself. . . . It is ignorance of the technique for experiencing the Being within oneself which is responsible for the misery in life.[21]

This "ignorance is sin," which is the basis of all suffering.[22] Sin is not a matter of personal responsibility for moral guilt for wrongs done. Sin is only a matter of ignorance of the "bliss-consciousness" of one's inner divinity. It is dealt with by a "technique for experiencing the Being within oneself" which is, of course, TM. It is claimed that if enough people practice TM all war, crime, violence, and human suffering will be remedied.

Man's ignorance of his divinity is dealt with by means of experiencing his divinity in "bliss-consciousness" so as to evolve into the impersonal state of "liberation." Thus Maharishi states that "the purpose of life is to enjoy bliss consciousness and evolve to the eternal state of liberation. . . ."[23] The "eternal state of liberation" is "Moksha," or Nirvana, which at death supposedly assures the fully enlightened meditator of his escape from personal existence into the ocean of "bliss-consciousness" which is "God." Thus Maharishi writes that for a "realized man . . . death is just a silent declaration of no return—no return to the cycle of birth and death."[24] The final purpose of personal life and individual consciousness, then, is its extinction in the impersonal and undifferentiated Ocean of Consciousness of Brahman. Breaking out of personal existence and escape from the thinking, acting, and loving possible as a personal being is the highest good for man, according to Maharishi. In his philosophy, a deep pessimism prevails as to the worth and fate of the personal. Personality is to be abandoned in favor of the impersonal. Relationships of love are to be abandoned forever in favor of an undifferentiated identity with the "All." The distinctively personal human functions of knowing, loving, and acting are overwhelmed by the nonhuman, the impersonal, and the impassive.

Because of his policy of concealing the religious aspects of TM, Maharishi does little public teaching about such obviously religious subjects as reincarnation and "Moksha," or liberation from the cycle of birth and death. They are, nevertheless, essential to understanding the fundamental reasons for practicing TM as Maharishi sees it. Though many are practicing TM for the lesser benefits of rest in ignorance of its spiritual tendency, the intended goal of TM is the supposed state of eternal but impersonal bliss.

THE BIBLICAL VIEW OF MAN

Maharishi's view of man as basically innocent was true of man's original state after the Creation, but it was put out of date long ago by the fall of man recorded in the third chapter of Genesis. Man had been created in the image of God and had lived for a time in a state of innocence. Man enjoyed a speaking relationship with his Creator until man chose a path of willful disobedience to the verbal command of God. The temptation that led to man's falling from his personal relationship with God was to be "like God." The serpent, representing Satan, told the woman that "when you eat of it [the fruit of the Tree of Knowledge] your eyes will be opened and *you will be like God, knowing good and evil*" (Gen. 3:5, RSV). It is significant that the serpent's offer of moral autonomy through knowing good and evil independently of God's Word is very similar to the promise made by Maharishi that "through this meditation right action spontaneously comes."[25] Maharishi's further claim that *man is God* was too gross a deception for Satan to try on beings (Adam and Eve) who had daily converse with their Creator. But now that man is separated from God by his presumption in trying to become like Him, man is subject to the even greater delusion that he is God. The enormity of the deception to which man became subject by his first step of independence from God is appalling.

The claim of human divinity is very ancient, then; but the Bible declares it to be false and exposes its source as Satan. God's response of judgment on the claim to divinity made by the prince of Tyre is recorded by the prophet Ezekiel:

> Thus says the Lord God: "Because your heart is proud, and you have said, 'I am a god, I sit in the seat of the gods, in the heart of the seas,' yet you are but a man, and no god, though you consider yourself as wise as a god . . . therefore, behold, I will bring strangers upon you. . . . They shall thrust you down into the Pit, and you shall die the death of the slain in the heart of the seas. Will you still say, 'I am a god,' in the presence of those who slay you, though you are but a man, and no god? . . . You shall die

the death of the uncircumcised by the hand of foreigners; for I have spoken, says the Lord God" (Ezek. 28:2, 6-10, RSV).

The "perennial philosophy" of pantheism of which Maharishi's Vedic monism is a special type, extends the claim to divinity from rulers to all men as a logical outgrowth of its confusion of Creator and creation through its premise of universal oneness. Thus the blasphemy of the prince of Tyre in view in the passage from Ezekiel is multiplied a billionfold. God's judgment against this claim to human divinity remains the same as that on Tyre because it denies and opposes the infinite, personal God and Creator who now sustains and who shall judge the world.

Man: A Creature

The Biblical account of man's creation shows that even when man was rightly related to the Creator, he was never of the same essence as God, as Maharishi believes. According to the Scriptures, "God created man in his own image ..." and "formed man of dust from the ground, and breathed into his nostrils the breath of life; and man became a living being" (Gen. 1:27; 2:7, RSV). The Creator/creature distinction here revealed is absolute and ineradicable in the Biblical view. Though he was not of the same uncreated essence as the uncreated Creator, man was made in the personal image of God so that God and man could have an "I-Thou" relationship of verbal communication and love. As long as man continued in willing obedience to the command that God gave him, man fulfilled his purpose of imaging or reflecting God's love and holiness in the visible creation.

Man's Problem

But man accepted the serpent's offer of moral autonomy and fell into the state of sinfulness the Bible describes. The psalmist David comments on the hereditary nature of man's sinful condition: "Behold, I was brought forth in iniquity, and in sin did my mother conceive me" (Ps. 51:5, RSV). The psalmist's words about his conception in sin and his birth in iniquity do not refer to the acts of his generation, but to his hereditary sinfulness by reason of the fallen state of the race of Adam. The prophet Jeremiah reveals the internal effects of man's fallen condition when he writes: "The heart of man is deceitful above all things, and desperately corrupt" (Jer. 17:9, RSV). The prophet Isaiah exposes the universal extent of sin in the external actions of men with his message that "all we like sheep have gone astray; we have turned every one to his own way" (Isa. 53:6, RSV). The New Testament sums up and confirms the prophetic word of the Old Testament in these words. "All have sinned and fall short of the glory of God" (Rom. 3:23, RSV). The gravity of sin is such that "the wages of sin is death ..." (Rom. 6:23, RSV).

Since the supreme God is holy and personal, man must give an account of himself to the Creator. Man suffers from real guilt for wrongdoing against his fellowman and against the God to whom he is personally responsible. The evidence of man's wrongdoing is his violation of the loving character of God, which he was created to reflect. Christ said that the two great commandments upon which all of God's law depended were to love God and one's neighbor. God's holiness and justice requires that He punish all sin against these imperatives to love.

Man's problem, then, is not his ignorance of his own (nonexistent) divinity, but his moral failure as a creature to love and obey his Creator. As a consequence, he fails to love his fellow creatures properly and suffers alienation from them as well as from God. The symptoms of the root condition of alienation of man from his Creator include also anxiety, boredom, sickness, and the fear of death. It is possible to treat these symptoms with apparent success for a time by meditation, but it does not deal with the underlying cause.

But God Himself has taken the initiative in providing a means for the reconciliation of Himself and the fallen race of man. God's means of reconciliation is not impersonal meditation but personal mediation. The Scriptures reveal the identity of the mediator in this passage: "There is one God and one mediator between God and men, the man Christ Jesus, who gave himself as a ransom for all ..." (I Tim. 2:5-6, RSV). The Second Person of the Trinity came to earth as a man in Jesus Christ, to live a perfect human life and to offer that life as a flawless sacrifice for the sins of men so that they might be reconciled to God. By trusting in what Christ has done by dying in their place for their sins, men can be reconciled to the loving and holy God. A talking relationship with God as a loving Father is restored and God's gift of eternal life in that relationship is granted to those who receive it by faith in the death of the Lord Jesus for their sins. By means of the sacrifice of His blood, Jesus has paid the debt for all the sins of the world, but only those receive the gift of life who receive the Savior as Lord.

By means of the mediation of the Lord Jesus Christ, God is restoring those who receive Christ as Lord to a personal relationship with Himself. Man's purpose in this relationship is to know, love, serve, and enjoy the Creator forever in the endless love of the Father, the Son, and the Holy Spirit, who together are the One, tri-personal God. In this relationship man comes once more to reflect the loving and holy character of the Creator as originally intended. In this function, man finds contentment and true fulfillment in the purpose for which he was created.

The contrast, then, between Maharishi's view of man's nature and purpose and the Bible's could hardly be more radical. Maharishi teaches that man is basically innocent in his inner nature. The Bible teaches that man's heart is deceitful and corrupt. Maharishi teaches that man is a divine being whose obvious sinfulness is the result of his ignorance of his own divinity. The Bible teaches that man is a creature of the personal God, and that he has, through willful disobedience, fallen out of his original state of imaging God's goodness. Maharishi teaches that by means of TM man can experience his own divinity and ultimately attain to a state of impersonal, bliss-consciousness forever. The Bible teaches that through faith in the death of Christ for his sins a man is reconciled to God and receives eternal life to be enjoyed in a resurrected and imperishable body in the personal presence of God forever.

The contrast is sharp at every point; but the difference in the ultimate fate of man according to the two views is worth particular note. In Maharishi's monism, man's purpose is to get out of personal existence as soon as possible. In Christian faith, man's purpose is to fulfill his personal existence in an endless love relationship with his personal Creator. This relationship can be restored immediately as soon as a person renounces his false claim to the divine attributes of autonomy and independence by calling upon Jesus as Lord and as Savior from sin.

When it is understood that man's deepest need is for personal relationships of love, it is clear that the Christian solution to man's problem of alienation from himself, from others, and from God must be chosen over the ultimate detachment from relationship of monism. Only through personal relationship with the infinite Person of the God of love can man be truly satisfied and God glorified for His goodness. Man's need is not for a system of meditation upon a transcendent, but impersonal, Being, but for personal mediation with the transcendent, personal God. Jesus Christ, the God-man, is the ideal mediator because in His Person He combines the transcendent and the finite, the divine and the human. He is the bridge between God and man who exposes the inadequacy of the impersonal techniques of meditation and of those personal but purely human leaders who offer "enlightenment" by means of such techniques. Christ's own claim to the unique function of mediator between God and man is simply: "I am the way—and the truth and the life. No one comes to the Father except through me" (John 14:6, NIV).

QUESTION: What does Maharishi think of Christ's atonement?

ANSWER: Maharishi's attitude toward Christ and His suffering is conditioned by his view of suffering in general which, in turn, depends on his view of "God" as the essence of all things. He asks, "This has been the question in my mind ever since I was young: God is omnipresent and God is almighty and God is merciful and in the heart of everyone, why should a

man suffer having God within himself?"[26] Why, indeed, should man suffer if he is divine? Maharishi
thinks that the answer is to reverse what religions
have told men—that man must be good in order to
know God. It is first necessary to "realize God" in
experience in order to be good. He therefore affirms
that

> being good is supposed to be the road to God. Now
> this is completely wrong. BECAUSE ONLY AFTER
> REALIZATION OF GOD CAN ONE BECOME
> GOOD.... All good in life is the result of contact
> with God. Only nearness to God, or with a good
> amount of God consciousness alone, could one be free
> from wrong.... THAT MEANS GOOD LIFE IS
> THE EFFECT, GOD REALIZATION IS THE
> CAUSE.[27]

Thus Maharishi has an insight into the basic defect
of all humanly originated religious systems, including,
finally, his own. They all attempt to raise man to the
level of God by means of man's works when what
man needs is a right relationship with God in order
to do good works. Maharishi fails to see that his own
system of consciousness raising to the level of God-
consciousness suffers from the same defect. His wrong
premise that "God is... in the heart of everyone"
leads him to believe that the solution to the problem
of evil and sin is a simple one requiring no suffering.
Just do TM, for "the path to God realization is this
meditation. Transcendental meditation is a path to
God."[28]

Maharishi challenges the Christian church sharply
on the point of religious experience. Perhaps he has
observed the spiritual deadness of some parts of the
professing church through the emptiness of the lives
of those of its members who have come to him for

fulfillment. Perhaps unconsciously, he rightly assesses the withering effect on spiritual life of Liberal and Existential theology (as well as dead orthodoxy) when he says:

> The whole field of religion is just left on the mental, on the basis of mental hallucination. Think, think, think, think, what is it? Thought of God is a thought of God, keep on thinking. You are thirsty, keep thinking of water, water, water, water and it does not satisfy the thirst. Thought of water is not water. No, it is not the thought of God that is going to help. It is the content of Godhead, it is our direct relationship with Him, it is our attunement with Him, it is our cognition of Him that is going to help.[29]

When Maharishi speaks of a "direct relationship" with God, he means the experience of one's supposed identity with the impersonal "God" through TM rather than a personal relationship with the personal Creator. Maharishi's critique of a large part of the professing Christian church is, nevertheless, accurate and devastating. It explains why many young people raised in Catholic and Protestant churches readily embrace TM. TM provides for them a religious experience that is perceptible and seems beneficial, whereas their church-based experience of prayer to God may have been quite empty. Through their church experience, such young people evidently have never responded to the life-challenging call of Jesus Christ, who said, "If you're thirsty, come to Me and drink. If you believe in Me, streams of living water will flow from you, as the Bible has said" (John 7:37-38, Beck).

Maharishi challenges Christian faith in another way by reinterpreting the Scriptures to make them support his view of suffering and God-realization. Thus he asserts in his conversational style that

> THIS IS THE BASIC FUNDAMENTAL OF SUF-
> FERING IN LIFE. No man, no Christian should ever
> suffer; because Christ, being his savior, has promised
> the Kingdom of Heaven is within you. People ask
> me about Christ and how can we find this teaching
> in the Bible? Bible teaches this, Vedas teach this,
> Upanishads teach this, Gita teaches this, Islam religion
> teaches this, Buddhism teaches this; this fundamental
> experience. What is necessary is this meditation. . . .[30]

The Bible takes a radically different view of suffering
from that of Maharishi as will be seen from the
Scriptures. Maharishi's reference to the kingdom of
heaven within should be met first, because it is so
frequently used by those influenced by Eastern
thought to affirm the inner divinity of man. But the
New Testament proclaims the divinity of only one
man, Jesus of Nazareth, who is God's only begotten
Son. Of the claimants to the divine title of Christ
(the anointed One of God) who preceded Him, He
said, "All who came before me are thieves and rob-
bers . . ." (John 10:8, RSV). Of those who would
come after Him making the same claim He warned,
"False Christs and false prophets will arise and show
great signs and wonders, so as to lead astray, if possible, even the elect" (Matt. 24:24, RSV).

The kingdom of heaven itself is the very subject
of the gospel of Christ and includes both the future
rule of God on earth through Christ in a visible kingdom at Christ's return and the present spiritual reality of the rule of God in the hearts and lives of
believers who have come into personal relationship
with the personal God as Father through faith in
Jesus Christ. For them alone does the prayer given
us by our Lord Jesus have present fulfillment of its
petition, "Thy kingdom come, Thy will be done, On

earth as it is in heaven" (Matt. 6:10). Genuine submission to God's will comes through receiving His Christ as Lord in a life-changing experience of spiritual rebirth (John 3:1-14). The real question for those who affirm the existence of an internal kingdom within man is, "Who shall rule that internal kingdom, the self (or Self) or the personal God and Father of the Lord Jesus Christ?" The Bible, then, teaches that only those who have become subject to Christ as Lord form part of the kingdom of heaven.

MAHARISHI'S VIEW OF SUFFERING

From his own basic premise of the universal oneness of divinity, Maharishi concludes that "the basic premise of every religion should be that man need not suffer in life."[31] For Maharishi, if everything is an emanation from the divine perfection of the Absolute, suffering lacks meaning. Given his premise, Maharishi would be right. The existence of suffering in the world may lead us to challenge either the reality of the world or the premise of universal divinity. The religions of the East have chosen the path of world denial in one form or another. For Maharishi the changing aspects of the world are not fully real but are "mithya," or phenomenal existence.[32] For the Christian, by contrast, the world is fully real and basically good because it is the creation of God. It is temporal, of course, but God has promised to renew it. The Christian doesn't seek to escape from the given reality of the creation because of his trust in the Creator for deliverance from change and decay into the unchanging and endless life of Jesus Christ who is "the same yesterday, today and forever" (Heb. 13:8).

THE CHRISTIAN VIEW OF SUFFERING

The other alternative is to acknowledge that man is not divine and is subject to suffering for the reason revealed in the Bible. Thus one may accept the testimony of his senses to the reality of the world and its suffering and the testimony of the Bible that gives a reasonable explanation for the existence of suffering. The Bible teaches that suffering entered the world with sin when man willfully chose to be autonomous from God by disobeying a command that God had given him. Man became subject to pain and physical death and actually experienced spiritual death in the loss of the communion with God, for which he was created. Man's suffering is a consequence of and punishment for his sin against God. But suffering has the redeeming purpose of calling forcefully to every man's personal attention that something is desperately wrong in the world. For after the sin and fall of man, God revealed His purpose of restoring man to a right relationship with God through the suffering of the coming Messiah (Christ), the seed of the woman (Gen. 3:15; Isa. 53). When man acknowledges to God that the thing wrong in the world is his own rebellion against God, reconciliation is accomplished by means of the sufferings for sin endured by Jesus.

The Book of Job reveals that the sufferings of the righteous are also a result of the conflict between God and Satan. God permits His servants to demonstrate that their faith in God transcends mere temporal rewards for their faithfulness. Finally, Job's "patience," or endurance, under the suffering of sudden loss of wealth, children, and health was rewarded by a twofold return of goods. The suffering he endured, however, so deepened his relationship with God who appeared to him and spoke to him that he repented for his own questioning of God during his suffering by saying, "I had heard of thee by the hearing of the ear, but now my eye sees thee; therefore I despise myself, and repent in dust and ashes" (42:5).

In the New Testament the redemptive character of suffering is made clearer by the sacrificial death of Christ. Christians are taught to rejoice in suffering for the sake of Christ and the gospel and for its purgative effect in their personal spiritual lives. In the Beatitudes, the sufferings of His disciples for His sake are singled out in this way:

> Blessed are you when men revile you and persecute you and utter all kinds of evil against you falsely on my account. Rejoice and be glad for your reward is great in heaven, for so men persecuted the prophets who were before you (Matt. 5:11-12).

The apostle Paul stresses the purgative and formative purpose of suffering when he affirms that "we rejoice in our sufferings, knowing that suffering produces endurance, and endurance produces character..." (Rom. 5:3-4). To the Philippians, Paul points out that suffering may be a privilege. He assures them that "it has been granted to you that for the sake of Christ you should not only believe in him but also suffer for his sake..." (Phil. 1:29). In the same letter he joins his longing to be like Christ to sharing in Christ's sufferings: Paul's desire is "that I may know him and the power of his resurrection, and may share his sufferings..." (Phil. 3:10).

The apostle also makes it clear that suffering is a universal experience for the Christian. He writes to Timothy that "indeed all who desire to live a godly life in Christ Jesus will be persecuted..." (II Tim. 3:12, RSV). For the Christian, then, suffering is so meaningful that it is to be confidently expected as the very cost of discipleship to Christ and endured joyfully as the means to sharing more deeply in His character. Only the personal presence of the living Christ in the lives of believers makes such an attitude possible. The attitude of ordinary Christians under persecution and martyrdom has from the beginning been one of the most convincing evidences of the reality behind the Christian hope of transcending death through resurrection with Christ.

MAHARISHI'S ATTITUDE
TOWARD THE SUFFERINGS OF CHRIST

With regard to the sufferings of Christ Himself, Maharishi's comment is:

> I don't think Christ ever suffered or Christ could suffer. The suffering man from the suffering platform sees the Bliss of Christ is suffering.... The suffering man sees a man and he sees him suffering. It's a pity that Christ is talked of in terms of suffering. It is a painless suffering. Those who count upon the suffering, it is a wrong interpretation of the life of Christ and the message of Christ. It is wrong. The One who says the Kingdom of Heaven is within, and that I and my Father are one—where is the question of suffering? The message of Christ has been the message of Bliss.... It's only the misunderstanding of the life of Christ, and we can understand that nobody can be held responsible....[33]

Actually, it is perfectly clear who is responsible for the idea that Christ's sufferings are transcendently important—Christ and His apostles are responsible. The apostle Peter affirmed, "I ... am also an elder, and a witness of the sufferings of Christ, and also a partaker of the glory that shall be revealed" (I Peter 5:1, AV). Peter pointed out that "what God foretold by the mouth of all the prophets, that his Christ should suffer, he thus fulfilled" in what Peter had witnessed (Acts 3:18, RSV). He clearly explains the transcendent meaning of Christ's passion as the ransom price for the lives of sinners when he writes, "For Christ also hath once suffered for sins, the just for the unjust, that he might bring us to God being put to death in the flesh, but quickened by the Spirit" (I Peter 3:18, AV).

The Christian Attitude
Toward the Sufferings of Christ

The apostle Paul affirms that he and other Christians share in the sufferings of Christ. He writes that "as we share abundantly in Christ's sufferings, so through Christ we share abundantly in comfort too" (II Cor. 1:5, RSV). Paul is not discontented in sharing Christ's sufferings. Indeed he writes to the church at Colossae, "I rejoice in my sufferings for your sake, and in my flesh I complete what is lacking in Christ's afflictions for the sake of his body, that is, the church..." (Col. 1:24, RSV). Before King Agrippa Paul affirmed, "I stand here testifying both to small and great, saying nothing but what the prophets and Moses said would come to pass: that the Christ must suffer, and that, by being the first to rise from the dead, he would proclaim light both to the people and to the Gentiles" (Acts 26:22-23).

Opposition to the prophetic teaching that Christ must suffer began from the moment He first revealed it to His disciples. From the following passage from the Gospel, the ultimate source of that opposition will become apparent:

> Jesus began to show his disciples that he must go to Jerusalem and suffer many things from the elders and chief priests and scribes, and be killed, and on the third day be raised. And Peter took him and began to rebuke him, saying, "God forbid, Lord! This shall never happen to you." But he turned and said to Peter, "Get behind me, Satan! You are a hindrance to me; for you are not on the side of God, but of men" (Matt. 16:21-23, RSV).

In denying the Biblical teaching that Christ really suffered in atoning for the sins of men, Maharishi, like Peter before the crucifixion, sides with Satan and man against God and Christ.

After Christ's resurrection, His response to those of His followers who were slow to perceive the necessity of His suffering, death, and resurrection was:

> O foolish men, and slow of heart to believe all that the prophets have spoken! Was it not necessary that the Christ should suffer these things and enter into his glory?" (Luke 24:25-26, RSV).

Later the Lord Jesus reminded the apostles that

> "These are my words which I spoke to you, while I was still with you, that everything written about me in the law of Moses and the prophets and the psalms must be fulfilled." Then he opened their minds to understand the scriptures, and said to them, "Thus it is written, that the Christ should suffer and on the third day rise from the dead, and that repentance and forgiveness of sins should be preached in his name to all nations, beginning from Jerusalem. You are witnesses of these things" (Luke 24:44-48, RSV).

To oppose the reality and necessity of the suffering

167

and death of Christ is to receive His rebuke and to side with Satan against God. Maharishi's denial of the sufferings of Christ is an attack upon the central teaching of the church of Jesus Christ and upon God's mightiest act of redemption for man. Maharishi himself must repent and receive forgiveness of sins if he is to escape God's judgment for his presumption. His followers also should seek God's forgiveness for their participation in an idolatrous system that denies the central fact of the gospel of Christ.

The necessity and supreme importance of the suffering and death of Christ is clearly established in the Scriptures. The Bible reveals the basis of the separation of God from man to be man's moral guilt before the holy and just Creator. That Jesus had to bear the infinite penalty of God's just wrath against sin on the cross in spite of His personal innocence is the definitive evidence that man's alienation from God is based on real, moral guilt. If man could be made pure or righteous by any other means, Christ's sufferings would have been superfluous and His agonized prayer, "O my Father, if it be possible, let this cup pass from me ..." would have been answered by a Yes. Neither would Christ have cried out from the cross, "My God, my God, why hast thou forsaken me?" But that is what He cried out because "God was in Christ, reconciling the world unto himself. ... For he hath made him to be sin for us, who knew no sin; that we might be made the righteousness of God in him" (II Cor. 5:19, 21, AV). Thus Jesus endured the pain of absolute separation from God and His grace like that of the damned in hell so that no one who submits to His Lordship need suffer such torment. Because Jesus Christ alone combined the infinite, personal nature of God the Son with the finite, personal nature of man, He alone was able to atone for man by bearing the infinite penalty of eternal separation from God in a finite period of time—the time He spent cut off from the love of God the Father while hanging on the cross under the burden of the sins of the world.

But the death of Christ was not the concluding event in the life of Christ as it is with other men. According to the Scriptures Jesus was raised from the dead the third day. Because Christ's sacrifice of His perfect life for the sins of men had satisfied God's just wrath against the rebellion of the human race, Jesus Christ was raised from the dead, and He Himself promised resurrection life to His followers. Thus the meaning of the death of Christ is the forgiveness of sins and eternal life for each one of His followers. In Christ's own words, His claim and promise are:

> I am the resurrection and the life. He who believes in me will live, even though he dies; and whoever lives and believes in me will never die (John 11:25-26).

The apostle Paul explains the way of receiving the salvation from death and hell that is resurrection life as follows:

> If you confess with your mouth, "Jesus is Lord," and believe in your heart that God raised him from the dead, you will be saved. For it is with your heart that you believe and are justified, and it is with your mouth that you confess and are saved (Rom. 10:9-10).

Because fallen man is separated from holy God as a sinner, salvation comes to man only through the suffering of another—the God-man, Jesus Christ. As Jesus said and supremely demonstrated in His own life, "Truly, truly, I say to you, unless a grain of wheat falls into the earth and dies, it remains alone; but if it dies, it bears much fruit" (John 12:24, RSV).

Notes

1. Maharishi, *The Science of Being and Art of Living*, rev. ed. (Los Angeles: International SRM Publications, 1967), p. 271.
2. Ibid., pp. 277 f.
3. Ibid., p. 276.
4. Ibid., p. 277.
5. Ibid., p. 278.
6. Ibid.
7. Ibid., p. 279.
8. Ibid., p. 273.
9. Francis A. Schaeffer, *He Is There and He Is Not Silent* (Wheaton, Ill.: Tyndale House, 1972), pp. 8-10.
10. Maharishi, *On the Bhagavad-Gita: A New Translation and Commentary* (Baltimore: Penguin Books, 1967), note 48, p. 441.
11. ———, *The Science of Being*, p. 269.
12. ———, *On the Bhagavad-Gita*, pp. 440 f.
13. ———, *The Science of Being*, p. 269.
14. Ibid., p. 274.
15. Ibid., p. 104.
16. Ibid., p. 276.
17. ———, *Meditations of Maharishi Mahesh Yogi* (New York: Bantam Books, 1968), p. 157.
18. ———, *The Science of Being*, p. 258.
19. ———, *Meditations*, p. 178.
20. Ibid., p. 177.
21. ———, *The Science of Being*, pp. 81 f.
22. ———, *On the Bhagavad-Gita*, p. 202.
23. ———, *The Science of Being*, p. 143.
24. ———, *On the Bhagavad-Gita*, p. 234.
25. ———, *Meditations*, p. 57.
26. Ibid., p. 61.
27. Ibid., pp. 58-59.
28. Ibid., p. 59.
29. Ibid., p. 64.
30. Ibid., p. 63.
31. ———, *The Science of Being*, p. 260.
32. Ibid., pp. 284 f.
33. ———, *Meditations*, pp. 123-124.

CHAPTER SIX

Transcendental Meditation: A Christian Response

by David Haddon

QUESTION: What about those Christian clergymen who practice and promote TM?

ANSWER: C. S. Lewis would be monumentally un-surprised by the hailing of Hindu monism in scien-tific guise as a new discovery by the theologically naïve dwellers in the post-Christian West. In *Miracles* he wrote as follows of pantheism in a historical per-spective that now seems strikingly prophetic:

> Modern Europe escaped it only while she remained predominantly Christian. . . . So far from being the final religious refinement, Pantheism is in fact the per-manent natural bent of the human mind; the perma-nent ordinary level below which man sometimes sinks . . . but above which his own unaided efforts can never raise him for very long. . . . It is the attitude into which the human mind automatically falls when left to him-self. No wonder we find it congenial. If "religion"

means simply what man says about God, and not what God does about man, then Pantheism almost *is* religion. And "religion" in that sense has, in the long run, only one really formidable opponent—namely Christianity. Modern philosophy . . . and modern science . . . have both proved quite powerless to curb the human impulse towards Pantheism. . . . Yet, by a strange irony, each new relapse into this immemorial "religion" is hailed as the last word in novelty and emancipation.[1]

The present relapse into this immemorial "religion" is novel, then, only in that it is often presented as science rather than as either religion or philosophy. Despite Lewis's insight into the seductiveness of pantheism to mankind in general, he might well be dismayed at the lack of theological definition and spiritual discernment that permits Hinduism to pass unchallenged by the clergy when it comes thinly disguised as science. The failure of those with pastoral responsibility to discern the practice of Hinduism from the practice of Christianity points to a poverty of both theology and spiritual experience in wide sections of the Christian church.

Specific examples of failure to discern the true, inner nature of TM by clergymen must be considered to correct such error and prevent others from being misled. The Christian response to failure on the part of leaders is to speak the truth in love in the hope that the erring ones may repent and that others may be warned against the error. Several Christian ministers and priests have written testimonials to the non-religious and beneficial character of TM. Reverend Patrick Mauney of Wickland, Rhode Island, for example, wrote a letter, dated December 26, 1974, to the chairman of the Naragansett School Committee encouraging the continued teaching of TM in Naragansett, Rhode Island, schools. Reverend Mauney writes:

> I am an ordained priest of the Episcopal church . . . and a practitioner of Transcendental Meditation. It is my opinion that there are no religious overtones to TM as presented. . . . I am happy to recommend TM as a technique of tremendous potential benefit to many, if not all, students in our schools . . . (SIMS reprint).

Another striking testimony by a clergyman to the value of TM appears in the *Christian Century* of December 10, 1975. Presbyterian Pastor John R. Dilley of Fairfield, Iowa (home of MIU), became a meditator in 1974 out of concern for a heart condition. He writes that:

> Our entire family have become meditators, and we have found no compromise in our commitment to Jesus Christ and to his church. Indeed, we have found that our entire life-style has become more Christian as we both give and receive love with less tension in our lives.

To the contention that TM is a form of religion, Rev. Dilley replies, "I would refute that claim categorically." He has instead accepted Maharishi's public contention that TM is a spiritually neutral technique equally applicable for Hindu and Christian.[2]

The testimonial letters by Christian clergymen published in *The TM Book* deserve special scrutiny because of their continuing potential to mislead a wide audience. The Reverend Karl E. Lutze, a Lutheran clergyman and professor of theology at Valparaiso University in Indiana, writes:

> I . . . had some initial reservations about TM from a

religious and theological standpoint. It was not without careful and serious study and reflection that I attempted to learn whether or not this art ... from the traditions of the Far East might be ... in conflict with my Christian faith. ... I do not find Transcendental Meditation an alternative to Christian faith; I practice it within the context of my Christian life. ... I regard meditation as another of God's good gifts to me. ...[3]

The other letter from *The TM Book* was written by a Roman Catholic priest, the Reverend Leo McAllister who is pastor of Immaculate Conception Church in Sacramento, California, and who was for six years chaplain of the California Assembly. He explains:

I am writing this letter to allay any fears, anxieties or misconceptions which Catholics may have concerning the practice of Transcendental Meditation. ... It is not a religion or a religious practice. ... I am happy to say that I can recommend it highly.[4] *

Another Roman Catholic priest who has written a testimonial letter for TM widely distributed by SIMS is Reverend Leo James Hoar, director of Notre Dame High School in Springfield, Massachusetts. His letter of January 7, 1974 was written "to recommend the

---

*In response to my inquiry as to whether the further information about TM now available had changed his opinion about it, Father McAllister sent me a copy of a letter he sent to TM headquarters. His letter of April 7, 1976 reads as follows:

A lot of harassment, many bothersome letters and calls and much confusion in the minds of many people, coupled with a tendency on the part of many TM practitioners to make a cult of following the Maharishi, make it necessary for me to ask you to please discontinue use of my letter endorsing TM. Please remove it from all centers and publications where possible.

I would like your confirmation that this has been complied with.

practice of Transcendental Meditation as a means of creating a more peaceful world and enjoying life more fully...." According to the "Springfield Republican" for March 24, 1974, Reverend Hoar approved a credit course in SCI for the fall of 1975 in the diocesan high school of which he is director.

These clergymen all appear to have been unknowingly deceived about the nature of TM. They almost certainly did not have knowledge of the material published in this book, as for instance, the text of the hymn of worship to Guru Dev used in the initiation ceremony. Part of the reason for their failure to discern the anti-Christian character of the *practice* of TM despite the initial misgivings of some of them was their accepting naïvely at face value the claims of Maharishi's representatives. Jesus warned us, however, that we are to be "as shrewd as snakes" as well as "innocent as doves" because He sends His disciples into the world "like sheep among wolves." Jesus also revealed this about the Christian's chief adversary, the devil: "When he lies, he speaks his native language, for he is a liar and the father of lies" (John 8:44, NIV). To be confronted by deception, then, is something every Christian should expect. By God's grace, no pastor need have been taken in by Maharishi's deception.

For those with pastoral authority, a failure to spiritually discern the true nature of a practice that exposes them and those entrusted to their care to idolatrous ritual is a serious matter, for "they keep watch ... as men who must give an account" (Heb. 13:17, NIV). Had their vague misgivings about TM been reinforced by a firm theological understanding like that of C. S. Lewis, of the *challenge of Christianity* to Eastern religion, neither TM nor any other pantheistic system based on the premise of human autonomy would have caught them unawares. Spiritual discernment, however, is also a matter of the work of the Holy Spirit in our lives stemming from an experience of spiritual rebirth that brings a person into a conscious, personal relationship with the Father through the mediation of Jesus Christ. It must be cultivated, of course, by a life of submission to the Lord Jesus Christ in obedience to His ministers in the church. Theological learning is never a substitute for knowing God; both theological learning and spiritual experience are needed to meet the challenge of missionary Hinduism in the post-Christian West.

QUESTION: How should a Christian respond to TM?

ANSWER: TM, as has been demonstrated in this book, is a religious practice that forms an integral part of a sect of missionary Hinduism. It produces faith in a false view of reality, which holds that man is divine in his inner nature and leads to an idolatry of both self-worship and guru-worship (of Guru Dev). TM itself is merely a typical representative of the spirit of Antichrist in the final quarter of the twentieth century. This spirit is ultimately responsible for the explosion of occult philosophy and practice into American and Western culture. This explosion is the result of a prior spiritual response on the part of man to God: the rejection of the light of the gospel in favor of philosophical and practical materialism. Materialism, having failed to satisfy man's need for spiritual experience, is now giving way before the more sophisticated deception of mystical experience as a means to fulfillment.

The range of occult philosophy and religion runs from (atheistic) Buddhism through the other Eastern religions, Bahaism, and Christian cults (such as Unity and Christian Science) to the magical arts of fortune telling, healing, and witchcraft. Scientology, EST, Eckankar, the sorcery of Carlos Castañeda's Don Juan, and various programs of developing psychic powers are other examples of the same underlying conviction that man is divine and should exercise divine powers. The common ground of occult philosophy and practice is the false "revelation" that man is a god or part of God. Maharishi himself strongly insists on this point of man's divinity (see pp. 149-152). The source of this deceptive "revelation" is Satan as was noted in chapter 5. I want to consider here three levels of response to TM as a typical representative of occult philosophy: the spiritual, the personal, and the political.

THE SPIRITUAL RESPONSE

The spiritual weapons the Christian possesses are described by the apostle Paul in Ephesians 6:10-20. These are the weapons that are needed in the conflict with the spiritual forces behind TM. The apostle makes it clear that the people ("flesh and blood," v. 12) who oppose us with false teachings about God are not our real opponents, but rather the Satanic spiritual forces who are blinding them to the truth of the gospel of Christ. In II Corinthians he explains that

> even if our gospel is veiled, it is veiled to those who are perishing. The god of this age [Satan] has blinded the minds of unbelievers, so that they cannot see the light of the gospel of the glory of Christ, who is the image of God. (4:3-4, NIV).

To effectively oppose these "spiritual forces of evil in

the heavenly realms" we must put on the full armor of God.

Paul describes the armor for this conflict as the belt of truth, the breastplate of righteousness, shoes of the preparation of the gospel of peace, the shield of faith, the helmet of salvation, and the sword of the Spirit which is the Word of God spoken (Greek, *hrema*). The purpose of the armor is to enable the Christian to stand by the power of God in the victory that Christ already gained by dying for our sins on the cross (Heb. 2:14-15; Col. 2:13-15; I John 3:8b).

The belt of truth represents the objective, propositional revelation of truth about God and man in the Bible. In the conflict with Eastern religions, the absolute distinction between Creator and creation (e.g., God and man) and the personhood of the supreme God are two particular points from the belt of truth that must be well understood and maintained. The breastplate of righteousness that protects us from self-condemnation and depression from guilt is basically the righteousness of Christ received by faith. It assures us of the forgiveness of our sins despite our unworthiness. The shield representing faith guards us from despair when under the attacks of the devil. To thank God for a painful situation and to praise Him in the midst of suffering is a way of wielding this shield because it expresses faith in God's sovereign goodness. Paul and Silas, for example, used this shield to good effect by singing praise to God in the jail at Philippi. The result was the opening of the entire prison and the conversion of the jailer to the Christian faith (Acts 16:16 f.). The helmet of salvation is the assurance that we are accepted by God so that whatever may happen to us in the conflict in this life, we will spend eternity with God in heaven

(I John 5:13). The sword of the Spirit is the Word of God as it is quickened to our lips to speak it to another person. The attachment of the sword to the belt of truth (the Word of God written) suggests the close relation of speaking God's message of the gospel of Christ to a firm grasp of the written revelation of the Bible.

After having taken up the full armor of God, Paul counsels us to join in the struggle by praying "in the Spirit on all occasions with all kinds of prayers and requests. With this in mind, be alert and always keep on praying for all the saints" (v. 18, NIV). Prayer is the ground upon which the spiritual battle is truly decided. Before taking action at the personal (evangelistic) level and at the political level, we should find out what God is doing by asking Him in prayer. He will provide us with direction that helps us to maintain a balanced attitude in the midst of conflict, along with a love for those who may count us as enemies because of our opposition to a false religious teaching that is claimed to be nonreligious.

Repentance and fasting are appropriate for those who want to intercede for the deceived and for the breaking of the influence of the "principalities and powers" of darkness. The emergence of Eastern religion and Western occultism from their semisecret status into the center stage of religious life in America is enough evidence of our need to fast and repent if we care about the spiritual and temporal fate of our country and her people. The rise of TM as a means of relaxation acceptable to middle-class Americans is a sign of advanced spiritual decadence as surely as is the acceptance of sexual immorality as normative.

Spiritual warfare requires these means because "though we live in the world, we do not wage war as the world does. The weapons we fight with are not the weapons of the world. On the contrary, they have divine power to tear down strongholds. We demolish arguments and every pretension that sets itself up against the knowledge of God, and we take captive every thought to make it obedient to Christ" (II Cor. 10:3-5, NIV). Before we approach the personal or political level of the conflict, our own spiritual life must be in order. Every thought must be brought into obedience to Christ. Obedience to Christ implies obedience to the ministers He has ordained in the church, for Christ said, "I tell you the truth, whoever accepts anyone I send accepts me" (John 13:20, NIV). Submission to spiritual and temporal authority in the church, the family, and in the state, worked out in practical obedience to those in authority, is prerequisite to success in spiritual warfare. Our example in this, as in all righteousness, is Christ, whose humility and obedience are presented to us in Philippians 2 as follows:

> Your attitude should be the same as that of Christ Jesus: Who ... made himself nothing, taking the very nature of a servant, being made in human likeness. And being found in appearance as a man, he humbled himself and became obedient to death—even death on a cross! ... Therefore, my dear friends, as you have always obeyed—not only in my presence, but now much more in my absence—continue to work out your salvation with fear and trembling ... (5, 7, 8, 12, NIV).

A Personal Response (Evangelism)

A personal response of loving concern for the meditator as a person is crucial to evangelizing those affected by the Eastern religious view that minimizes the importance of personal existence. By demonstrating real personal concern for the meditator, a Christian can make a theological point without argument: persons *are* important. When the opportunity arises, the Christian can explain *why* persons are so important—because God Himself is a Person. Impersonal methods of sharing the gospel such as literature distribution should be joined to personal encounter, to emphasize the basic truth that God is personal.

For those already in the habit of sharing their faith (those whose feet are already well shod "with the preparation of the gospel of peace") only a few special points need to be made. First, don't waste time trying to convince a meditator that TM is religious. He may be so defensive of his hundred-dollar investment or so delighted by the novel experience of meditation that he will be unconvinced by any evidence you offer. It is better to let this point be made by means of literature that the meditator can examine in privacy where his ego is less exposed to injury. It may be helpful, however, to nudge the conscience of an instructor of TM, who knows very well that he must conceal the true nature of the initiation ritual everytime it is discussed, by questioning him about why the Hindu Trimurti of Brahma, Vishnu, and Shiva are worshiped in the ritual under the form of Guru Dev.

By all means share your personal testimony to the life-changing experience of receiving Jesus as Lord and of your speaking relationship with the personal Father which you continue to experience through Christ. The meditator may identify with you as a person who values spiritual experience. He will tend to assume that in some way you have gained an inkling of the same experience of transcendence he enjoys more fully by TM. At this point you may simply confront your friend with Christ's claim to be the unique God-man and the only mediator between God and man (John 14:6; Matt. 11:27; I Tim. 2:5). The problem of sin as real moral guilt before the personal God and Creator and as the reason for Christ's suffering and death in our place is a way of presenting the essential point of man's sinfulness. The blood atonement of Christ offers the meditator something undreamed of in Maharishi's system: the forgiveness of sins. An in-depth presentation of the gospel to one deceived by the occult philosophy of human divinity may require more than usual emphasis on the fallen condition of man set forth in Romans 1 through 3. Because the entire system is based on a complete confusion of the Creator with His creation, the point of the absolute distinction between God and man must also be emphasized (Rom. 1:25).

It is not necessary, therefore, to become fluent in the high abstractions of Eastern religion to share your faith with a meditator. It *will* be necessary to love the meditator enough to listen carefully to what he has to say, thus demonstrating that you regard him as a person worthy of your attention. As you listen with "your loins girded about with truth," you will gradually become aware of the points of agreement and disagreement between Eastern religion and the Christian faith. Use the points of agreement (e.g., the existence of an invisible supreme Being, the importance of spiritual development, the fact that man as he is has a problem) as springboards to bring in the Biblical teaching on points of disagreement (God personal, rather than impersonal; man a dependent creature, rather than an autonomous spark of the divine essence; sin as moral guilt before God, rather than an ignorance of inner divinity). Even if in discussion a meditator seems to win all kinds of debater's points against you, avoid argument and let the Holy Spirit maintain a peaceful and loving attitude as you continue to share from the authority of Scripture his need for the Savior. If your peace is a fruit of the Spirit, its genuine quality will be apparent even to those who have been deceived by the false peace of meditation. Above all, love your meditating friend and regard him as the object of God's love. The gospel message of God's love and forgiveness requires a loving messenger.

A Political Response

In the political arena, there are issues raised by TM (and other forms of occult religious practice) at local, state, and national levels. At the local level, public school courses in SCI and TM and other uses of public funds to promote TM should be challenged by local Christian leaders. Presentation of the text of the *puja* (pp. 47-50) together with the SIMS requirement that all who learn TM attend a ceremony where this hymn to the Hindu divinities is sung to Guru Dev as their manifestation is convincing evidence of the religious nature of the practice. The juxtaposition of Shankara's Hindu doctrines with the essentially identical teaching of SCI as cited in chapter 3 is convincing evidence of the religious basis of the teaching. Concerned local pastors can take advantage of their public status as religious authorities to take the initiative in demonstrating the religious character of TM before public bodies and to the news media. They should prepare objective statements challenging the SIMS claim to a nonreligious status for SIMS and TM.

Christians should devote some serious thought not

only to their response to TM but also to the underlying problem of the schools that has caused school administrators to accept an alien religion in disguise as a promising measure. The superficial symptoms of the problem are student drug use, student violence, and student apathy to learning. The underlying cause of students' undisciplined behavior and their lack of motivation is the secularization of society, which has left parents and children alike without meaning or purpose in life beyond self-gratification. The exclusion of religious observances from the schools is only a reflection of the practical exclusion of God from the everyday life of the American people. National repentance, rather than school reform, is the urgent necessity.

The need for religious training to provide discipline and purpose in the lives of students, nevertheless, is desperate. The movement to provide some teaching about religion in public schools through courses such as the Bible as literature is a primitive step in this direction. Courses in which representatives of various religious groups are permitted to explain their teachings and practices are another. It is not surprising that TM, various other forms of yoga, and even astrology and witchcraft are being taught in the spiritual vacuum of the public schools of a society that has turned its back to God.

The brightest prospect for educational improvement on the horizon is the growing impetus of the Christian school movement. In recent years the rate of starting new schools under Christian auspices has been encouraging. A political measure that would foster this movement while providing greater educational opportunity for the poor and greater equity in bearing school costs should be considered by Christians.

The proposal is that a voucher for the amount of money appropriated by government for each student be made available to all parents who then may present the voucher to the' school of their choice, public or private. This progressive step would enable poor parents and others with religious convictions to educate their children in the religion of their choice—a luxury now largely reserved for the well-to-do. It would enable poor parents dissatisfied with public schools to choose another option—religious or not. It would provide simple equity for those parents who are presently bearing the dual burden of paying taxes for a public school system and of paying tuition for their children who are attending private schools. Christian schools stand to be in the forefront of the already growing movement toward quality private education that such a measure would encourage.

Given the present lack of a public religious consensus and the essential relation between education of the young and religious training, this form of government encouragement of private education may be the best practical solution to the concrete problems of drug abuse, violence, and nonlearning in the schools. The uncritical acceptance by some school administrators of TM as a means to solve the present impasse of secularized education points up the critical nature of the problems faced by our schools. Recitation of slogans about the separation of church and state is only an evasion of reality. The materialist and evolutionary philosophy of the present educational establishment is essentially a religious view of the world.

Under the present system the government is thus subsidizing anti-Christian presuppositions about the nature of reality. That an enterprise as important as the public education of our youth is carried forward without any explicit reference to God impresses on the mind of the student the message that God is either nonexistent or unimportant. Giving the parents the option, through the voucher proposal, of choosing the religious presuppositions under which their children are to be educated would extend religious freedom by liberating students of the present public school system from the tacit assumption of God's irrelevance.

Aside from the positive step of promoting government measures that would encourage private education, Christians need to remain alert to oppose resolutions favoring TM, SCI, and MIU at the state and national level. As long as SIMS keeps trying to promote these resolutions, letter-writing campaigns against them will be needed to let legislators know (as happened recently in New Jersey) of the substantial public opposition to government support for TM.

As mentioned in chapter 1, legal action is proceeding against TM and the federal government with an eye to gaining a definitive Supreme Court ruling against the teaching of SCI and TM in public schools. Should that suit prove successful, further litigation in the schools may prove unnecessary. The situation with regard to the consumer-fraud suit investigation in Iowa is different. Even if a court ruling against TM for fraudulent advertising is obtained in Iowa, that will have no effect beyond the borders of Iowa. Consumer-fraud suits need to be started in each of the forty-nine other states. The basis of the suit is SIMS advertisement of TM as nonreligious even though initiation requires attendance at a religious ritual in which Hindu gods are worshiped and homage is paid to Guru Dev as a manifestation of these gods. Legal counsel must be obtained locally, of course, but specific information, documentation, and advice is available from Spiritual Counterfeits Project, P.O. Box 4308, Berkeley, California 94704. The Spiritual Counterfeits Project is an arm of the Berkeley Christian Coalition (formerly Christian World Liberation Front).

When involved in political controversy and even if confronted by lying and slander, the Christian is to love his opponents. This is no ideal option, but a command of the Lord Jesus Christ. His word calls for the transcendent reaction of joy in suffering persecution. Jesus said, "Blessed are you when people insult you, persecute you, and falsely say all kinds of evil against you because of me. Rejoice and be glad, because great is your reward in heaven, for in the same way they persecuted the prophets who were before you" (Matt. 5:11-12, NIV). If a Christian is not willing to avail himself of God's grace to give him a loving attitude toward his enemies in political controversy, it would be better for him to avoid temptation by not engaging in political action at all, "for the wrath of man worketh not the righteousness of God" (James 1:20).

Finally, the Christian must avoid what the psalmist warns against in the first verse of the first psalm—he must not sit in the seat of the scornful. Though the Christian bears the revelation of the ultimate truth about God and reality, he must not be scornful of those who do not yet share in this truth. The heart of the Christian response to TM must always be a genuine concern for the people deceived by it. Only then will the response be truly worthy of the followers of the One who commanded us to love God, to love our neighbor, to love one another, and to love our enemies.

QUESTION: If meditation is not the way to God taught by the Bible, just what is the way to the God of the Bible?

ANSWER: The Bible says that "there is a way which seemeth right to a man, but the end thereof are the ways of death" (Prov. 14:12, AV). Meditation and the techniques of mystical enlightenment are intended to be ways of raising man's consciousness to the level of God. This way of attaining to Deity along with all other ways of gaining a good status before God by our own efforts may seem good to us as men, but they all end in death because they do not please God. The Bible reveals that man's consciousness cannot be raised to the level of God—"For my thoughts are not your thoughts, neither are your ways my ways, saith the Lord. For as the heavens are higher than the earth, so are my ways higher than your ways, and my thoughts than your thoughts" (Isa. 55:8-9, AV). The distinction between Creator and creature thus is as absolute in the realm of consciousness as it is in substance.

God's thoughts about man's salvation are so different from man's that they are based on a principle that excludes man's works (whether of meditation or of morality) from consideration *as means to reach* God. The principle that God applies to man's salvation is called "grace." In practice it means that salvation is not and cannot be earned; instead it is an absolutely free gift of love to undeserving men. The Scripture says that "the wages of sin is death, but the gift of God is eternal life through Christ Jesus our Lord" (Rom. 6:23, NIV). God's principle of salvation for man is directly stated by the apostle Paul as follows:

> *It is by grace* you have been saved, through faith—and this not from yourselves, it is the gift of God—*not by works,* so that no one can boast (Eph. 2:8-9, NIV, emphasis added).

This principle of grace—God's giving of salvation to men as an undeserved gift—is a necessity in view of man's fallen nature (see pp. 152-158). Man is a sinner separated by his rebellion and disobedience from the holy God. The prophet Isaiah reveals that it is sin that separates man from God when he says that

> your iniquities have made a separation between you and your God, and your sins have hid his face from you so that he does not hear. For your ... lips have spoken lies, your tongue mutters wickedness (Isa. 59: 2-3, RSV).

The prophet shows the futility of our efforts at self-made righteousness in that "we are all as an unclean thing, and all our righteousnesses are as filthy rags" (Isa. 64:6, AV). Isaiah condemns the autonomy of the self of man under the figure of the straying sheep, declaring that "all of us like sheep have gone astray, each of us has turned to his own way ..." (Isa. 53:6a, NAS).

The essence of man's sinfulness is his claim to autonomy for the self, whereas, in reality, he is a dependent creature. The claim of human autonomy reaches its peak in the yogi who affirms the divinity of the self. The yogi (such as Guru Dev or Maharishi), who is considered to have attained divinity, is locked into a system based on establishing righteousness by means of works or "action." Maharishi, indeed, attributes salvation to action—the action of meditation. He writes that

> this verse [*Bhagavad-Gita* 3, 20] extols action ... as a means to eternal liberation from bondage. ... Meditation itself is an activity. In view of this, it can certainly be held that it is "action alone" that brings perfection.[5]

The Biblical principle of grace says that "faith alone" saves from sin, for "not by works of righteousness which we have done, but according to his mercy, he saved us" (Titus 3:5, AV).

As a consequence of man's sinfulness before the God of holiness, man is under God's judgment. Paul warns that "because of your stubbornness and your unrepentant heart, you are storing up wrath against yourself for the day of God's wrath, when his righteous judgment will be revealed" (Rom. 2:5, NIV). God is a just judge who will not forever tolerate the violation of His loving character, which is what sin really is. Because God loves men (John 3:16) He has provided a way of escape for sinners. That way of escape is the Lord Jesus Christ. Because He was God made flesh (John 1:1, 14), He was able (as man) to represent man before God and also (as God) to receive the infinite punishment deserved by the human race during the finite period of time He spent bearing the wrath of God against sin on the cross.

The central point of Christ's suffering is that it was done for the sake of others—for those who receive the gift of salvation from Him. The prophet Isaiah, writing hundreds of years before Christ, foresaw that

> he was wounded for our transgressions, he was bruised for our iniquities; upon him was the chastisement that made us whole, and with his stripes we are healed. ... The Lord has laid on him the iniquity of us all.

> ... By his knowledge shall the righteous one, my servant, make many to be accounted righteous; and he shall bear their iniquities. Therefore I will divide him a portion with the great, and he shall divide the spoil with the strong; because he poured out his soul to death, and was numbered with the transgressors; yet he bore the sin of many and made intercession for the transgressors (Isa. 53:5, 6b, 11b, 12, RSV).

Because Christ has already suffered the penalty for sin—the spiritual death of utter separation from God and His grace—salvation is freely offered to sinners on the basis of faith in Christ's death for their sins. This faith means trusting entirely in Christ for salvation rather than in our own goodness. Accepting this kind of a gift is a humbling experience, because it requires the admission that as sinful men we have nothing with which to recommend ourselves to God. It also involves a total commitment of our lives to Jesus Christ as Lord. God's Word, the Bible, and Christ's Spirit must become the standards for our entire lives. Anything displeasing to Christ and God must be surrendered in order to receive the gift of eternal life.

After receiving the free gift of salvation, obedience to Christ will require us to follow His example of humility in receiving water baptism, for the Scripture commands us to "repent and be baptized, every one of you, in the name of Jesus Christ so that your sins may be forgiven" (Acts 2:38, NIV). Participation in the fellowship of a vital church is another necessity, for the Scripture says, "Go in pursuit of integrity, faith, love, peace *in fellowship* with those who call upon the Lord out of pure hearts" (II Tim. 2:22, MLB). Again it exhorts against "forsaking the assembling of ourselves together..." (Heb. 10:25).

191

Neither baptism nor church attendance are conditions of salvation, for salvation is by faith alone; but an unwillingness to do either may indicate a refusal to obey Christ as Lord. Christ's challenge to potential followers is:

> If anyone would come after me, he must deny himself and take up his cross daily and follow me. For whoever wants to save his life will lose it, but whoever loses his life for me will save it (Luke 9:23-24, NIV).

For those who count the cost and determine to devote their lives to Jesus as Lord, a prayer such as the following is a good way to begin fellowship with the Son of God and, through Him, with the Father:

> Lord Jesus, I know that I am a sinner. I have done many things I knew were wrong. But I know that because You loved me You died for my sins on the cross in my place. I ask You to forgive me for all my sins. Please come into my heart and life as my Lord, my Master. Amen.

Since Jesus promises to acknowledge to God and His holy angels those who are not ashamed to acknowledge Him to sinful men, tell one person of your commitment to Christ as your Lord right away. Then begin to read the New Testament to build your faith in God. Pray to the Father in Jesus' name or directly to Jesus for guidance and help all the time. If you do something you know is wrong, stop doing it and confess it to God as a sin. Then thank Him for forgiving you according to His Word which says, "If we confess our sins, he is faithful and just to forgive us our sins and to cleanse us from all unrighteousness" (I John 1:9). This verse should be learned by heart, because we need to be sure that our sins are forgiven in order to keep our fellowship with God free and open. Begin looking for a church where the love of Christ and His place as Lord are evident. Trust God to guide and protect you by His great love (Prov. 3:5-6).

QUESTION: What should a Christian who had practiced TM or a meditator who has just become a Christian do to be free of the influence of TM?

ANSWER: Meditators are taught that even if a person discontinues practicing TM, he will certainly come back to it eventually. I talked with one ex-meditator who was disturbed by the suggestion that he might go back to the practice of TM, because he had never liked it at all. The thought that some unseen influence might cause him to get back into TM caused him anxiety. After he became a Christian, however, he no longer worried about it because of his confidence that in Jesus he had all he needed. Another former meditator, however, reported that even after becoming a Christian for some time after quitting TM she had a fear of the people she had associated with in meditation. These examples show that a spiritual practice such as TM may have lingering psychological effects. To minimize these and other disturbing effects over the long run, it is necessary to deal with the spiritual roots of such effects.

Three points need to be considered about the spiritual effects of TM. First, the spirit of TM is fundamentally opposed to Christ, as evidenced by Maharishi's denial of Christ's suffering for the sins of the world (see p. 165). Second, the initiation ceremony of TM involves the meditator in an idolatrous worship ritual. Third, involvement in anti-Christian teaching

193

and idolatrous practice opens a person to the influence and harassment of, and even control by, evil spirits.

A Christian who wants to be free from the influence of TM after practicing it for a time should renew his confession that Jesus is his Lord, and this should be done both privately in his heart in prayer to God and verbally before at least one witness. A non-Christian meditator who wants to get out of TM should do the same with the understanding that such a confession is a lifelong commitment to obey Christ as Lord which will bring him into personal relationship with God. For anyone who says, "I confess that Jesus is Lord," as an act of submission to the will of God, Christ opens the door to forgiveness of sins and to the exercise of the authority of His name.

To be completely free from the spiritual influence of an occult spiritual system such as Maharishi's TM, one must come fully under the authority of the Lord Jesus Christ, because God has delegated His authority to Jesus. Therefore, Jesus declares that "all authority in heaven and on earth has been given to me" (Matt. 28:18). On making this announcement, Christ immediately delegated this authority on earth to His disciples, giving them authority to make disciples, to baptize them, and to teach them to obey His commands (Matt. 28:19). Christ's authority is still found on earth in the ministers He has established in the church. A person who wants to be free from evil spiritual influences, therefore, should seek out a pastor, who is himself subject to Christ, and other delegated authorities in the church, and submit himself personally to that pastor to be strengthened in the faith and built up in Christ. Having subjected himself to Christ and to Christ's delegated authorities in the church, the Christian can then freely exercise the authority of the name of Jesus to banish evil spiritual influences from his life.

As was pointed out earlier, TM involves every meditator in the sin of idolatry. When a Christian becomes aware of it, the Holy Spirit will convict him of the need to repent. The sin of idolatry should be confessed to God and forgiveness should be received by faith (I John 1:9). Thanksgiving for this forgiveness and for the atoning blood of Jesus which makes it available will be a natural outflow. A person should make a clean sweep by confessing all occult contacts such as astrology and fortune telling as well as drug use and habitual sexual sins such as homosexuality and masturbation. A meditator who had dabbled in astrology, for example, might pray: "Father, I confess the sin of idolatry that I committed in TM. I confess my sin of unbelief in seeking hidden knowledge about myself based on the signs of the zodiac and by consulting my horoscope. Thank you, Lord Jesus, for forgiving me and cleansing me with Your blood according to Your Word." Satan, as the accuser of the brethren, is silenced by this application of the blood of the Lamb, for it is written, "they overcame him by the blood of the lamb . . ." (Rev. 12:11; see also Exod. 20:3-6 and Deut. 18:10-14 for God's viewpoint on idolatry and occultism).

The next step is to renounce all of the sins you have confessed and to destroy the associated books and occult objects (see Acts 19:18-20). A practicer of TM, for example, might just say, "I renounce TM and the mantra I was given and Maharishi in the name of the Lord Jesus Christ."

The confession of Jesus as Lord, the confession of

all occult practices as sin, the renunciation of those practices, and the destruction of the associated books and objects are important in themselves as acts of obedience to God and of resistance to the devil (James 4:7). They also serve as a necessary preparation for standing against the "principalities and powers" by exercising the authority of the name of Jesus.

The Lord Jesus Himself delegated authority over the demons even before the outpouring of the Holy Spirit on the church at Pentecost. He told the seventy who rejoiced because "even the demons submit to us in your name" that he had given them "authority to trample on snakes and scorpions, and to overcome all the power of the enemy . . ." (Luke 10:17, 19, NIV). Now, however, the entire body of Christ shares in the authority of the Head, for "God raised us up with Christ and seated us with him in the heavenly realms in Christ Jesus . . ." (Eph. 2:6 NIV). In Christ, then, the church is seated "in the heavenly realms, far above all rule and authority, power and dominion . . ." (Eph. 1:20-21, NIV).

Jesus in His temptation and Paul in his encounter with a spirit of divination demonstrate the exercise of the authority over Satan and demons now granted to the church. Jesus said, "Go away, devil! It is written: 'Worship the Lord your God, and serve Him only'" (Matt. 4:10, Beck). Paul said, "In the name of Jesus Christ, I command you to come out of her!" (Acts 16:18b, NIV).

In the same way, the Christian can exercise the authority of the name of Jesus against any oppressing spirits who may have gained a foothold through TM or another occult or sinful practice. Following the Biblical examples, he should say, "In the name of

Jesus Christ, I command Satan and the spirits of TM to go away." There may or may not be some physical manifestation of the presence of evil spirits. Should the Christian experience feelings of depression, confusion, or indifference to God soon after this procedure, he should continue to stand in the victory of Christ by testifying to the "overcoming power of the blood of Jesus" (Rev. 12:11). Ray Stedman of Peninsula Bible Church in Palo Alto, California, considers that depression, confusion, or indifference to God in the life of a Christian are sure signs of spiritual warfare.

Appropriate Scripture passages, such as Colossians 2:1-15 and Ephesians 6:10-18, should be read, memorized, meditated on, and obeyed in order to help fill any vacancy in the spiritual life of the believer with the life of the Lord Jesus. Specific passages, such as Matthew 4:10 and Revelation 12:11, should be memorized for use against the devil when he brings evil thoughts into the mind during spiritual warfare. Prayer and praise to God and fellowship with other believers must be maintained. If spiritual oppression was present and relief is obtained, it is important for the Christian to maintain a proper relation of submission and obedience to spiritual and other authority. Otherwise the same problem may recur.[6]

QUESTION: How does Christian faith differ from TM with regard to fulfillment in life?

ANSWER: Christian faith and TM differ in their means to fulfillment as the impersonal differs from the personal. Maharishi describes TM as the "mechanical path to God realisation...."[7] Certainly, the repetition of a mantra until consciousness is depersonalized through the suspension of memory and thought is mechanical and impersonal. And having begun a spiritual pursuit on the impersonal path of mantramic meditation, the meditator naturally tends to come to an impersonal conclusion about the nature of God. The conclusion that God is not a person is built into the impersonal technique of reciting a word to yourself to the point of meaninglessness, for the only possible way for a man to get to know the invisible Person of God is for them to communicate in words meaningful to both.

Christian faith, therefore, pursues personal fulfillment in God by personal means of communication, such as Scripture reading and prayer. By reading the Gospels, for example, one learns that Jesus Christ is called the divine Word and that He taught His disciples (but *not* the multitudes) to talk to God as Father in simple but rationally significant words—for example, those of the Lord's Prayer (Matt. 6:7-13). In this definitive teaching on prayer, Jesus specifically rejected repetitive verbal exercises such as TM as a means to God when He said, "When you are praying, do not use meaningless repetition, as the Gentiles do" (Matt. 6:7, NAS). For those not yet His disciples, Christ presented Himself as the personal way to the personal Father (Matt. 11:27-30; John 14:6).

The question of whether the Supreme Being is a personal God or an impersonal Being is of the greatest practical importance in the quest for personal fulfillment. By denying the personhood of God, Maharishi minimizes the importance of personality and denies the ultimate survival and significance of persons. In contrast, the Christian acknowledgment of God as the Person in whose image man was created maximizes the importance of persons. The Biblical promises of resurrection of the body, of judgment, and of eternal reward in heaven or eternal punishment in hell all imply the significance and eternal duration of human personality. Christ's bodily resurrection from the dead is evidence of His deity and of the Father's acceptance of His sacrificial death for the sins of men. It also establishes the survival of personality beyond the grave. Thus Christ's resurrection provides objective grounds for confidence in the ultimate triumph over sin and death promised to His followers.

Through the forgiveness of sins that it brings, faith in Christ also provides deep rest for the mind and body of those burdened by alienation and guilt. According to the Bible, alienation from and moral guilt before the personal God whose holiness is absolute are man's basic problems. The anxiety and stress that TM relieves are mere symptoms of the insidious underlying disorder the Bible calls "sin." Sin at its root is man's willful refusal to acknowledge and serve the personal God and Creator as supreme (Rom. 1:18-25). The pantheist's denial of personality to the Supreme Being is thus an expression of sin. Men can be liberated from this innate tendency to disregard the Person of God, however, because one day about A.D. 30, Jesus Christ suffered the penalty of death for our sin in our place on a cross a short distance outside of Jerusalem.

Because He arose from the dead the third day, Jesus still calls to us, "Come to me, all who labor and are heavy-laden, and I will give you rest" (Matt. 11:28, RSV). The rest that Christ offers reaches to the very root of our beings by healing our alienation from God. That is why the apostle Paul can write to believers: "Once you were alienated from God and were enemies in your minds because of your evil behavior. But now he has reconciled you by Christ's physical body through death to present you holy in his sight" (Col. 1:21-22, NIV).

Just as the impersonal can never explain the existence of the personal, neither can a person find his complete fulfillment in the impersonal experience of Eastern meditation. Fulfillment in life is achieved in a personal relationship of love with the personal Father through His only Son, Jesus Christ of Nazareth. Such a relationship is begun by the *personal act of speaking* to the Lord Jesus in faith while turning away from the self to God in heaven. By thus acting in faith on the basis of the *objective,* written record of what God has done in Christ for the redemption of man, one makes the *subjective* discovery that he has become a son of God (John 1:12; Gal. 4:6). Intellect and experience are integrated by this relationship with the Creator who made both mind and body.

A full comprehension of the Person of Jesus Christ, then, depends on both an intellectual understanding of the revelation of Scripture about Him and a personal experience of spiritual rebirth through Him. Then we can grasp the Biblical revelation of Jesus Christ as God Incarnate—the Creator and Sustainer of the universe made flesh. A majestic passage of Scripture that so reveals Christ says of Him:

> He is the image of the invisible God, the firstborn over all creation. For by him all things were created: things in heaven and on earth, visible and invisible, whether thrones or powers or rulers or authorities; all things were created by him and for him. He is before all things, and in him all things hold together. And he is the head of the body, the church; he is the beginning and the firstborn from among the dead, so that in everything he might have the supremacy. For

> God was pleased to have all his fullness dwell in him,
> and through him to reconcile to himself all things,
> whether things on earth or things in heaven, by mak-
> ing peace through his blood, shed on the cross (Col.
> 1:15-20, NIV).

In the same Epistle, the apostle Paul warns against those who deny that the divine fullness is to be found only in Christ, saying, "See to it that no one takes you captive through hollow and deceptive philosophy, which depends on human tradition and the basic principles of this world rather than on Christ" (Col. 2:8 NIV). Only the concrete personal fullness of Deity that is Christ can be the wellspring of fulfillment for mankind, "for in Him all the fullness of the Godhead dwells bodily, and in Him ... you are enjoying fullness of life" (Col. 2:9-10, MLB).*

The ultimate goals of Christian faith and TM differ as sharply as the means to those goals and in precisely the same way—as the personal from the impersonal. The final goal of TM becomes, for those who attain to Cosmic-consciousness and beyond, "liberation" (Moksha) at death from personal existence into the impersonal ocean of Being. Many meditators, of course, are unaware that they have embarked on a dynamic spiritual path whose end is the loss of personhood in the impersonal "Absolute"; but the ultimate goal of TM is just this extinction of personal life. Thus there is a discontinuity as the personal life of the yogi or meditator is supposed to be swallowed up into the impersonal at death. The individual soul suffers total annihilation of memory, feeling, knowl-

---

* From *Transcendental Meditation* by David Haddon. © 1975 by Inter-Varsity Christian Fellowship and used by permission of Inter-Varsity Press.

edge, and will. All personal relationships of love are thus permanently dissolved.

The personal goal of Christian faith involves no such discontinuity. Personal existence and personal relationships will endure forever. And the sacrifice of Christ redeems completely—man's body as well as his soul. Jesus' word of promise is "that everyone who looks to the Son and believes in him shall have eternal life, and I will raise him up at the last day" (John 6:40).

Although there is complete continuity of life in relationship with God and with fellow believers, the Christian looks forward to a greatly increased scope in life through the elimination of the limitations of mortality and through the perfection of our imperfect knowledge of God. The apostle Paul prophetically describes the opening into new vistas of life at the second coming of Christ for both the dead and the living as follows:

> Listen, I tell you a mystery: We shall not all sleep [die], but we shall all be changed—in a flash, in the twinkling of an eye, at the last trumpet. For the trumpet will sound, the dead will be raised imperishable, and we shall be changed. For the perishable must clothe itself with the imperishable, and the mortal with immortality. When the perishable has been clothed with the imperishable, and the mortal with immortality, then the saying that is written will come true: "Death has been swallowed up in victory."
>
> "Where, O death, is your victory?
> Where, O death, is your sting?"
>
> (I Cor. 15:51-55, NIV)

The perfection of our knowledge of God at Christ's coming is also described by the apostle:

> Now we see but a poor reflection; then we shall see face to face. Now I know in part; then I shall know fully, even as I am fully known (I Cor. 13:12, NIV).

The experiential knowledge of God in view here will thus be full and complete with the return of Christ.

In conclusion, then, TM promises you the ultimate extinction of thought, feeling, and will—complete loss of personality and the permanent severing of all love relationships. Instead of personhood, there is simply the impersonal ocean of "bliss-consciousness." According to the Scriptures, these promises of TM are both false and unworthy of man's dignity as a being made in the image of God. They obscure the real danger of eternal punishment in hell as well as the joyous prospect of eternal life in heaven.

Christian faith promises you an eternal life of conscious, personal communion with God and with all other believers. Through the Holy Spirit, this relationship is a present experience to be brought to final perfection at Christ's return in glory and power. Through the word of the gospel and the Spirit of Christ, this promise of unending personal communion with God still reaches to every person who will receive Jesus Christ as Lord and Savior.

Notes

1. C. S. Lewis, *Miracles* (New York: Macmillan, 1947), pp. 84 f.
2. John R. Dilley, "TM Comes to the Heartland of the Midwest," *Christian Century*, Dec. 10, 1975, pp. 1131 f.

3. Denise Denniston and Peter McWilliams, *The TM Book* (Allen Park, Michigan: Versemonger Press, 1975), p. 18.

4. Ibid., p. 17.

5. Maharishi, *On the Bhagavad-Gita: A New Translation and Commentary* (Baltimore: Penguin Books, 1967), p. 213.

6. Pat Brooks, *Using Your Spiritual Authority* (Monroeville, Pennsylvania: Banner, 1973), pp. 103 f.

7. Maharishi, *The Science of Being and Art of Living,* rev. ed. (Los Angeles: International SRM Publications, 1967), p. 304.